The Smithsonian Book of Presidential Trivia

The Smithsonian Book of Presidential Trivia

Amy Pastan

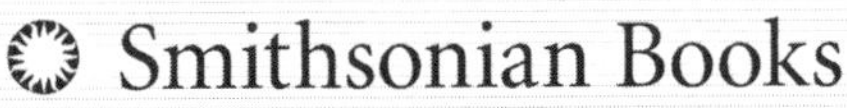

Smithsonian Books
WASHINGTON, DC

This book may be purchased for educational, business, or sales promotional use. For information, please write:

Special Markets Department
Smithsonian Books
P. O. Box 37012, MRC 513
Washington, DC 20013

Published by Smithsonian Books
Director: Carolyn Gleason
Production Editor: Christina Wiginton

Smithsonian Advisory Committee, National Museum of American History, Political History:
Harry R. Rubenstein, Lisa Kathleen Graddy,
William L. Bird, Debra Hashim

Compiled and written by Amy Pastan
Foreword by Marc Pachter

Edited and designed by Kensington Media Group
Editorial Director: Morin Bishop
Design: Barbara Chilenskas

Library of Congress Cataloging-in-Publication Data
Pastan, Amy.
The Smithsonian Book of Presidential Trivia / Amy Pastan.
p. cm.
Includes bibliographical references and index.
ISBN 978-1-58834-325-3 (alk. paper)
1. Presidents—United States—Miscellanea. I. Title.
E176.1.P3929 2012
973.009'9—dc23

2012022435

Manufactured in the United States of America
16 15 14 13 12 5 4 3 2 1

Contents

Not So Trivial Trivia

NO ONE REALLY KNEW WHAT A PRESIDENT WAS BEFORE George Washington reluctantly agreed to accept the office after the passage of the Constitution. The document itself was of little help because it gave paltry guidance as to the proper role of a chief executive in the government of the new nation. Monarchs were mostly the way of the Europeans and it was the European models that our nation's founders wanted to avoid.

So what was a young nation to do? Essentially they said, "Let George do it," then watched as he defined just what a president should be. It was the regal yet not power hungry Washington who demonstrated how one might be both head of state and head of government; who demonstrated that one might and indeed should relinquish power after two terms; and who balanced authority with a sense of connection to the aspirations of individual Americans.

And was he a tough act to follow! His successor, John Adams, was the first president to be mocked because he didn't get that balance right. Indeed, all the successors that followed Washington into this great office have experienced, in differing degrees, a combination of reverence for the president they have become (having previously been mere politicians) and suspicion that they are mortal after all, and need to be reminded of that.

Because we adore the presidency but not always individual presidents, we as a nation are continuously fascinated with who each of these men (so far, only men) were before the office, are while in the office, and become after the office. It is hard to imagine a more interesting fate for an American citizen. And so we want to know everything about our presidents and continue to talk about them, with reverence and irreverence, even after they are long gone.

And now we have a book that encapsulates that curiosity and passion we all share, and not surprisingly it is the Smithsonian that has taken on the challenge. We ask many things of the Smithsonian as we explore the extraordinary questions and seek the incredible objects and icons that define our shared American experience. So much of that concerns and illuminates the American presidency, in its grandeur and in its humanity.

In this one volume, *The Smithsonian Book of Presidential Trivia*, you will find questions you have asked and those that others have wondered about. Who was the first president born in a log cabin? Which president was a tailor in his early life? Who is the only president to hold a patent? Which president waited until he was in his sixties to cast his first vote?

The Smithsonian Book of Presidential Trivia also provides an opportunity to peer inside the vault of Smithsonian presidential treasures. You won't be surprised at how many of the objects collected since the Smithsonian's origins in the nineteenth century have to do with the president's official role, but you may be surprised to learn how many have to do with what might be called the private and personal side of the presidency. We have called this a book of presidential trivia because we want to suggest the breadth of our interest in the presidency. But we also know that in fact nothing concerning the presidents is truly trivial. It is all important, all interesting to us as Americans. And in that sense, we are all historians, all curators. I was just one of the ones lucky to get to do it full time at the Smithsonian.

Marc Pachter
Director Emeritus,
National Portrait Gallery
Interim Director,
National Museum of American History

Chapter 1

Citizens, Officers, Heroes, and Saviors

THE COLORFUL LIVES OF OUR LEADERS

"The qualities of a great man are 'vision, integrity, courage, understanding, the power of articulation, and profundity of character.'"

—*Dwight Eisenhower*

Q: How many generals became president and who are they?

A: *Twelve: George Washington, Andrew Jackson, William Henry Harrison, Zachary Taylor, Franklin Pierce, Andrew Johnson, Ulysses S. Grant, Rutherford B. Hayes, James Garfield, Chester Arthur, Benjamin Harrison, and Dwight Eisenhower.* Even before becoming United States commanders in chief, these men served their country in the military. The president with the highest rank is George Washington, who was general and commander in chief during the Revolutionary War. In 1976 President Gerald Ford posthumously promoted Washington to "General of the Armies of the United States" and specified that he would forever rank above all officers of the United States Army, past and present.

Officer's coat and waistcoat worn by General Washington, 1770s-1780s.

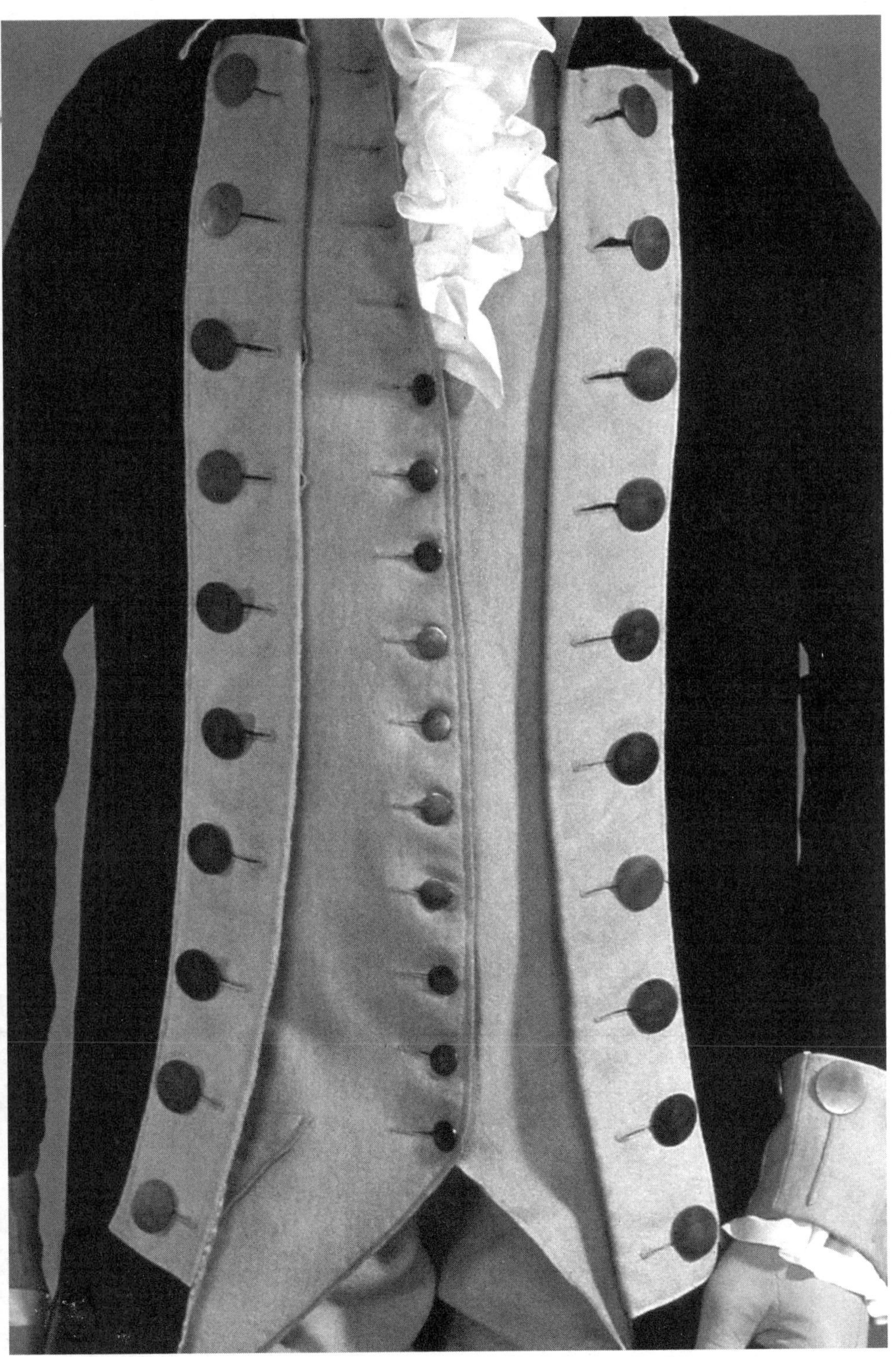

Q: **Which president was the first to throw out the ceremonial first pitch of the baseball season?**

A: *William Howard Taft.* As a child Taft loved the game of baseball. His large girth made it difficult for him to be a competitive base runner, but he was a good hitter. Taft threw out the first ball of the season on opening day 1910, and in doing so started a long tradition of presidential participation in the national pastime. He was, however, unable to attend the Washington Senators opener in 1912 because he was mourning the loss of his dear friend and military aide, Major Archibald Butt, who had died in the *Titanic* disaster.

Taft's opening day toss to Washington Senators pitcher Walter Johnson, April 14, 1910. Butt is standing beside the president, at right.

Q: Which president liked to skinny dip in the Potomac?

A: *John Quincy Adams.* Ironically, the most sober and seemingly straight-laced president was also the one who shed his clothes each morning to take a refreshing plunge into the Potomac River. Adams's forays to his favorite swimming hole were not without incident. He once had a servant row him out to the far bank so he could swim back. A passing storm caused the boat to capsize in the middle of the river, leading the most powerful man in America to fear for his safety.

Q: Which president did not vote until he was in his sixties?

A: *Zachary Taylor.* As an on-the-move career army officer, Taylor did not vote in an election until 1848. He had no official residence and no inclination to divulge his political leanings. Few knew that the soldier and slave owner was also a strong nationalist who as president would work to preserve ties between the North and South and oppose the expansion of slavery into western lands.

Q: Which president once co-owned a major league baseball team?

A: *George W. Bush.* Bush was a minority owner of the Texas Rangers from 1989 to 1998. Aside from his financial stake in baseball, Bush was a life-long lover of the sport. He was a catcher on his West Texas Little League team, played in prep school, and briefly pitched during his freshman year at Yale University, although he confessed, "I was not a reliable starter."

Q: Who was the only former president to later serve in the Senate?

A: *Andrew Johnson.* After his tumultuous presidency came to an end in 1869, Johnson returned to his home state of Tennessee and remained active in the Democratic Party. He ran unsuccessfully in various congressional elections but was eventually elected to the U.S. Senate in 1874, becoming the only former president to serve there. In his only speech from the senate floor, Johnson denounced Ulysses S. Grant's reconstruction policy. He died from a stroke in 1875.

Q: Which president was a peanut farmer?

A: *Jimmy Carter.* Carter grew up on a peanut farm near Plains, Georgia. Although he left home to study nuclear physics and serve in the navy, he returned there after his father's death to look after the family business. The man with the southern drawl and wide grin seemed a long shot for the presidency, but the public liked his down-home style. Peanut imagery proliferated throughout his successful campaign.

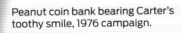

Peanut coin bank bearing Carter's toothy smile, 1976 campaign.

Who was the first president to be born outside the forty-eight continental states?

A:

Barack Obama. Obama was born in Honolulu, Hawaii, on August 4, 1961. His father and mother, who met at the University of Hawaii, divorced in 1964. His mother remarried an Indonesian student, and the family moved to Jakarta in 1967. Obama returned to live in Hawaii with his maternal grandparents from 1971 until his graduation from high school in 1979. Of his childhood, Obama has written, "The opportunity that Hawaii offered—to experience a variety of cultures in a climate of mutual respect—became an integral part of my world view, and a basis for the values that I hold most dear."

Souvenir hatchet commemorating the centennial of Washington's inauguration, 1889.

Q: Is the story of George Washington and the cherry tree true or false?

A: *False.* The famous tale of Washington and the cherry tree was the fabrication of Mason Weems (1759–1825), who added the story to the fifth edition of his book, *The Life and Memorable Actions of George Washington* (1806). In Weems's fanciful telling, the young Washington mortally wounded his father's cherry tree with a hatchet. When confronted about his crime, he replied, "I cannot tell a lie, Pa; you know I can't tell a lie. I did cut it with my hatchet." Weems included the tale to illustrate Washington's honest nature and to promote book sales.

Q: Who was the first president born in a log cabin?

A: *Andrew Jackson.* Jackson was born into poverty in 1767 in the backwoods of the Carolinas. His Irish father died before he was born, and his mother passed away when he was fourteen. Despite these disadvantages, he became a lawyer, planter, and general. His presidential campaign drew on the log cabin as a symbol of the common man and allowed Jackson to connect with ordinary citizens. In fact, Jackson was so invested in the power of the people that he liberally used his presidential veto to protect Americans from their own government. This earned Jackson the wrath of Congress and many political enemies, but secured him loyal voters who saw to his reelection.

Snuffbox depicting Jackson as a military hero, 1828.

Q: Which president signed legislation establishing the Smithsonian Institution?

A: *James Polk.* On August 10, 1846, Polk signed legislation founding the Smithsonian Institution and ended more than a decade of debate within the Congress, and among the general public, about how to implement an unusual bequest from English chemist and mineralogist James Smithson, who never set foot in the United States. When Smithson died in 1829, he left a will stating that his estate should go to the United States "to found at Washington, under the name of the Smithsonian Institution, an establishment for the increase and diffusion of knowledge."

Q: Which president's name at birth was Leslie King?

A: *Gerald Ford.* Ford was originally named for his biological father, Leslie Lynch King Sr., a wool merchant from Omaha, Nebraska, who married Ford's mother, Dorothy Gardner, in 1912. Dorothy fled her abusive husband soon after Ford's birth, and in 1916 remarried. Her new husband, a salesman in a family-owned paint store in Michigan, was named Gerald R. Ford. Leslie was renamed Gerald R. Ford Jr. His new father, a businessman and active Republican, had a strong influence on the future president.

Q: Who was the only divorced president?

A: *Ronald Reagan.* Reagan's first marriage to actress Jane Wyman, with whom he had appeared in the film *Brother Rat* (1938), ended in divorce in 1948. In 1952 he remarried another actress, Nancy Davis. Actor William Holden was the best man at their wedding. The Reagans appeared in one film together in 1957 before Nancy retired from acting to raise their children; he would act for another eight years before embarking on a career that took him to the presidency.

Which president was the owner of a profitable whiskey distillery?

A: *George Washington.* Whiskey was one of Washington's most important business ventures at Mount Vernon. At peak production in 1799, the distillery used five stills and a boiler and produced eleven thousand gallons of whiskey. With sales of $7,500 that year, it was perhaps the country's largest distillery. Washington's plantation manager James Anderson, a Scottish man with distilling experience, urged him to start the venture, which was also an efficient way to use unsold ground wheat, corn, and rye.

Q: Who was the tallest president?

A: *Abraham Lincoln.* At six feet four, a fraction of an inch taller than Lyndon Johnson, Lincoln holds the height record for presidents. At only 180 pounds, he was gangly, with disproportionately long arms and legs. His law partner commented, "His eyebrows cropped out like a huge rock on the brow of a hill; his long sallow face was wrinkled." Not a pretty picture. But the Great Emancipator seemed to accept his physical shortcomings and was even known to joke about them.

Black broadcloth office suit worn by Lincoln during his presidency, c. 1860–65.

Q: Which president became a Supreme Court justice after his retirement?

A: *William Howard Taft.* A graduate of Yale and Cincinnati Law School, Taft loved law but was unsure about politics. At the urging of his wife, Nellie, and mentor, Theodore Roosevelt, he reluctantly accepted his party's nomination for the presidency in 1908, calling the presidential campaign "one of the most uncomfortable four months of my life." After losing the 1912 election to Woodrow Wilson, Taft served as a professor of law at Yale and was later appointed by Warren Harding as chief justice of the United States, a post he considered his greatest honor.

Q: Who was the only president who never married?

A: *James Buchanan.* When Buchanan was twenty-eight years old he was engaged to Anne Coleman of Lancaster, Pennsylvania. The two quarreled, and she broke off the engagement. Shortly afterward, she died—an apparent suicide. Her family blamed Buchanan for the tragedy, and he never forgave himself. "I have lost the only earthly object of my affections," he said, "without whom life presents to me a dreary blank." Indeed, Buchanan never filled the void with another woman and threw himself into politics to escape his grief. During his presidency, his niece Harriet Lane served as White House hostess.

Q: Which president was nicknamed Old Rough and Ready?

A: *Zachary Taylor.* Taylor had a distinguished military career, first as a commissioned lieutenant, then as a captain in the War of 1812, a colonel in the Black Hawk War of 1832, a brigadier general in the Second Seminole War from 1837 to 1840, and as a general in the Mexican-American War from 1846 to 1847. It was during the Seminole War that his men—inspired by his disheveled appearance and unpretentious manner—assigned Taylor the moniker Old Rough and Ready. In the election of 1848, after leading the United States to victory in the Mexican-American War, Taylor's heroism and his catchy nickname won him votes.

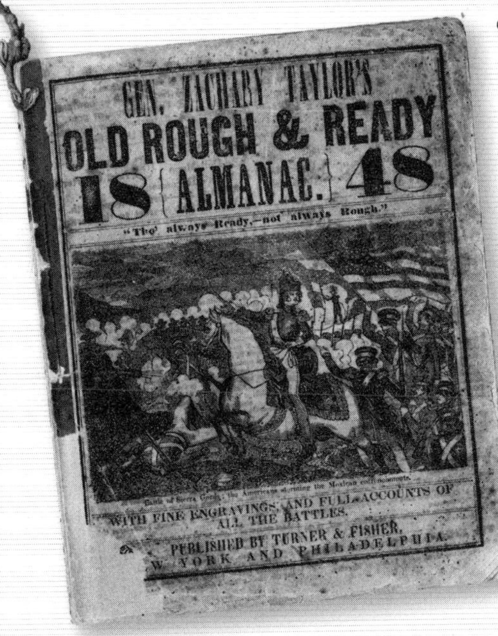

Almanac celebrating Taylor's victories in the Mexican-American War, 1848.

Q: Who was the only president to hold a U.S. patent?

A: Abr*aham Lincoln*. On May 22, 1849, Congressman Lincoln received a patent for his method of lifting boats over shoals. Lincoln was inspired to create such a device during a visit to Niagara Falls, where he saw a grounded boat moved from the shallows by forcing empty barrels under its sides. His patent model, now in the Smithsonian, was produced with help from Walter Davis, a mechanic from Springfield, Illinois. The patent was issued but the invention was never produced.

Lincoln's patent model for lifting boats over shoals, 1849.

Q: **Which president was a tanner in his early life?**

A: *Ulysses S. Grant.* Grant's father was a tanner by trade, and young Ulysses was often called on to work in the tannery, a job he detested: the blood-soaked hides made him gag. But Grant, a skilled horse-handler, gladly helped to haul wood, plow fields, and reap the harvest. His horsemanship served him well throughout his military career.

Q: **Which presidents owned slaves?**

A: *George Washington, Thomas Jefferson, James Madison, James Monroe, Andrew Jackson, Martin Van Buren, William Henry Harrison, John Tyler, James Polk, Zachary Taylor, Andrew Johnson, and Ulysses S. Grant.* Interestingly, eight of the twelve owned slaves while they held office, including Washington, Jefferson, Madison, Monroe, Jackson, Tyler, Polk, and Taylor. Four of the first five presidents were from Virginia, then the largest slave state in the United States. Washington had between 250 and 300 slaves. Jefferson, who authored the Declaration of Independence, had approximately 200. Madison owned about 100 slaves, and Monroe about 75. Grant became a slaveholder through his marriage to Julia Dent, whose family owned a plantation outside of St. Louis. Grant's family so abhorred the practice of slavery that they refused to attend his wedding.

Q: Which president had a brief career as a cowboy?

A: *Theodore Roosevelt.* A sickly boy who suffered from asthma, Roosevelt became a firm believer as an adult in the benefits of exercise. When his first wife, Alice Lee, died in 1884, the grieving widower traveled to the Dakota Badlands to become a cowboy. A tougher man moved back to New York two years later and lit up the political arena with his energy. As chief executive, this outdoorsman and hunter created the first four federal game reserves.

Chaps worn by Roosevelt on his Dakota Territory ranch, 1884–86.

Q: Who was the only non-Protestant elected president?

A: *John F. Kennedy.* Kennedy was Roman Catholic and there was much talk during his presidential campaign (mostly by the Protestant clergy) about whether his allegiance would be to his Pope or his country. The candidate was quick to confront the issue. In a speech to the Greater Houston Ministerial Association, Kennedy said, "I believe in an America where the separation of Church and State is absolute, where no Catholic prelate would tell the President (should he be Catholic) how to act and no Protestant minister would tell his parishioners for whom to vote."

Q: Which president was offered professional football contracts by the Detroit Lions and Green Bay Packers after college?

A: *Gerald Ford.* Ford was a star center for the South High Trojans football team in Grand Rapids, Michigan. At the University of Michigan he grabbed the spotlight as a senior, when he was named most valuable player for the Wolverines and appeared in the 1935 Chicago Charities College All-Star Game against the Chicago Bears. Soon after, he was offered the opportunity to go pro, but opted to study law instead. He coached football at Yale before becoming a full-time law student there.

Q: Who was the oldest president to enter the White House?

A: *Ronald Reagan.* Reagan was sixty-nine when he was inaugurated president of the United States. While some questioned whether he was up to the job, he met the demands of the office for two terms and even survived an assassination attempt. Known for his self-deprecating humor, Reagan joked, "Thomas Jefferson once said, 'We should never judge a president by his age, only by his works.' And ever since he told me that, I stopped worrying."

Q: Which president was called the Great Engineer?

A: *Herbert Hoover.* Hoover earned a degree in geology from the newly opened Stanford University and was managing mines in Australia by the age of twenty-three. After marrying Lou Henry, the couple moved to China, where Hoover served dual roles for the Chinese Imperial Bureau of Mines and for his British employers, Bewick, Moreing and Co. Hoover's success earned him the title of Great Engineer, as well as great wealth. Both a brilliant businessman and a millionaire, he was the people's choice for president in 1928, but he lost their confidence after the stock market crash of October 1929.

Q: Who was the only former president to later serve in the House of Representatives?

A: *John Quincy Adams*. In November 1830, twenty months after leaving office, Adams was elected to represent Massachusetts in the U.S. House of Representatives. During his seventeen-year tenure in Congress, he supported the anti-slavery movement and promoted the establishment of the Smithsonian Institution. The well-educated but humorless Adams was considered a much more effective congressman than president. He held office right up until his death at the age of eighty.

Ivory cane given to Adams by abolitionist supporters in 1844.

Q: **Which president was once the youngest Navy pilot in the armed forces?**

A: *George H. W. Bush.* When Bush got his wings in World War II, he was the youngest pilot in the United States Navy. He enlisted on his eighteenth birthday and eventually flew fifty-eight combat missions. On one mission over the Pacific, he was shot down by Japanese anti-aircraft fire and recued by a U.S. submarine. He received the Distinguished Flying Cross for his bravery.

Veterans for Bush button, 1992, with image of the president wearing his Navy jacket.

Q: How many presidents received the Nobel Peace Prize and who were they?

A: *Four: Theodore Roosevelt, Woodrow Wilson, Jimmy Carter, and Barack Obama.* Roosevelt received his in 1906 for his many efforts toward international peace, including his role in formulating the 1905 peace treaty between Russia and Japan. Wilson was awarded the Nobel in 1919 for founding the League of Nations after World War I. Carter was long retired from the presidency when he won the prize in 2002 for his efforts to advance human rights and achieve peaceful solutions to international conflicts. Obama was honored with a Nobel in 2009 for his work toward strengthening international diplomacy and cooperation.

Q: Which president used his stature as the Hero of New Orleans to gain national fame?

A: *Andrew Jackson.* The feisty, frontier-born Jackson earned this lofty title for his role in defeating the British army in a famous battle during the War of 1812. His successful campaign for and election to the office of the presidency proved that leaders with military prowess appealed to the electorate. The seventh president was the second battlefield commander after George Washington to become commander in chief.

Q: **Who was the first in a long line of lawyers to become president?**

A: *John Adams.* Like many other early presidents, Adams was apprenticed as a lawyer after college. It wasn't until later in the nineteenth century that it became customary to have a law school degree. Twenty-five of our nation's forty-four leaders have had legal training.

Q: **Which president popularized the term "OK"?**

A: *Martin Van Buren.* Van Buren was born in Kinderhook, New York. After he went into politics, he became known as Old Kinderhook. It is said that the term "ok" is based on this nickname, although the expression may have already existed and Van Buren's moniker simply increased its popularity. The original usage could have been an abbreviated and intentionally misspelled stand-in for "all correct."

Q: **Who was the first African American president?**

A: *Barack Obama.* Obama's mother was a white American from Wichita, Kansas, and his father was a black African from Kenya. The president was born in Hawaii, but spent much of his childhood in Indonesia. As a candidate Obama confronted the issue of race and said he hoped his election would break barriers for other Americans of color.

Button made to commemorate Obama's inauguration as the forty-fourth president of the United States.

Which president rose early to practice piano?

Harry Truman. Truman often said that if he'd been good enough to be a professional pianist, he never would have become president. From the age of ten he was a devoted music student, rising at five a.m. to play for two hours before school. He stopped taking lessons at the age of fifteen, when he realized that he did not have the talent to make it as a concert musician. Still, Truman loved to play. At the National Press Club canteen in 1945, when he was still vice president, Truman was photographed at the keyboard, serenading actress Lauren Bacall, who gazed seductively at him from the top of the upright.

Which president was a popular Hollywood film star before entering politics?

Ronald Reagan. The handsome son of an Illinois shoe salesman, Reagan did not follow in his father's footsteps. After college he worked as a radio announcer, and in 1937 he headed out to Hollywood to work for Warner Brothers. Reagan made more than fifty movies for the big screen. Among his co-stars were his first wife, Jane Wyman, and his second wife, Nancy Davis. He later became head of the Screen Actors Guild, a dress rehearsal for his future roles as governor of California and president of the United States.

Q: Which president had the largest shoe size?

A: *Warren Harding.* Harding wore a size fourteen. Unfortunately, those big feet did not ensure that his administration would be on firm footing. It turned out that Harding's trusted advisors were not so trustworthy, and his presidency was riddled with scandal. He died before his term was complete, and his wife burned his potentially incriminating correspondence. However, his stately slippers and sporty golf shoes survive at the Smithsonian.

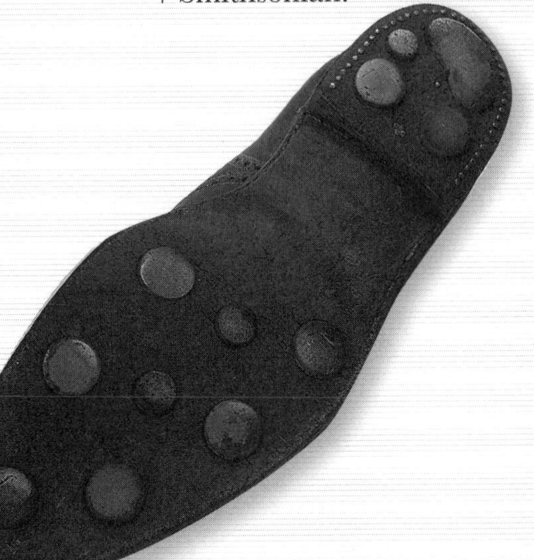

Shoes worn by avid golfer Harding, c. 1922.

Q: Who was the only president to serve in both World War I and World War II?

A: *Dwight Eisenhower*. Eisenhower graduated from West Point Military Academy in 1915 and was already a commissioned officer by the time the United States joined the fighting forces in Europe during World War I. However, Eisenhower remained stateside in that conflict, serving as a commander of the tank training center at Camp Colt, Pennsylvania. Eisenhower held the rank of brigadier general by the time the United States entered World War II in 1941. In December 1943 President Franklin Roosevelt named him supreme allied commander, with orders to mount an invasion of Europe. After the success of D-Day, Eisenhower was promoted to five-star general. He accepted Germany's surrender on May 7, 1945.

General Eisenhower's summer dress uniform, c. 1943–45.

Q: **Which presidents were speed-readers?**

A: *John F. Kennedy and Jimmy Carter.* Kennedy could allegedly read 1,200 words a minute. In 1954–55 he and his brother Bobby attended meetings at the Foundation for Better Reading in Baltimore. He later brought teachers from the Evelyn Wood Reading Dynamics program into the White House to help increase the reading speed of his top-level staff members. In addition to JFK, Carter also took a speed-reading course at the White House with his family and several staffers. While Nixon's personal reading speed is not reported, he also promoted the Evelyn Wood program to members of his staff.

Q: **Which president was a fashion model in his youth?**

A: *Gerald Ford.* Ford's first love was a woman named Phyllis Brown, a gorgeous blond who became a fashion model. Brown persuaded Ford to invest in a modeling agency and to do some modeling himself. Together they appeared in a ski resort spread for *Look* magazine (1940) and on a cover of *Cosmopolitan* (1942). Ultimately, the pair broke up. She wanted to continue modeling in New York, and he decided to forego the runway and begin his law career.

Q: Which president weighed the most?

A: *William Howard Taft.* The twenty-seventh president fought a life-long battle with his weight. As a school kid, he was unflatteringly nicknamed Big Lub. As president, he reached 332 pounds. After getting stuck in the White House bathtub, he ordered one custom-made to accommodate his generous bulk. His new tub was seven feet long and forty-one inches wide; four average-sized men could sit in it. On leaving the presidency Taft began to count calories and managed to shrink down to about 250 pounds, a much healthier weight for his six-feet-two-inch frame.

Q: Who was the first president to be born an American citizen?

A: *Martin Van Buren.* Van Buren was born on December 5, 1782, in Kinderhook, New York. All seven previous presidents were born British subjects. Their births predated the Declaration of Independence and the American victory in the Revolutionary War. Van Buren was the descendant of Dutch immigrants. The family spoke Dutch at home, making English Van Buren's second language.

Q: Which battle-tested president was sickened at the sight of blood?

A: *Ulysses S. Grant.* It turns out that the man called Unconditional Surrender Grant during the Civil War was a squeamish guy when it came to the sight of blood—at least animal blood. He ate his steak well done and never touched fowl. As a child growing up in rural southern Ohio, he was the rare boy who did not hunt game for sport. In fact, Grant did not fit the stereotype of a hardened soldier. He was modest, soft-spoken, seldom used profanity, and disliked dirty jokes.

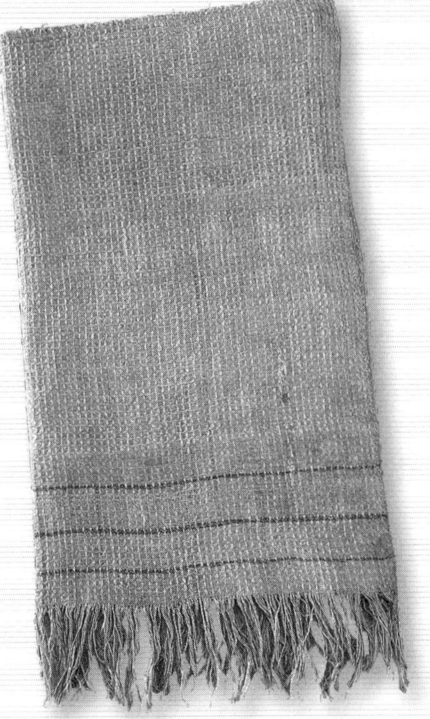

Towel used as truce flag by Confederate troops during General Lee's surrender to Grant at Appomattox, 1865.

Q: Which president was a tailor in his early working life?

A: *Andrew Johnson*. The seventeenth president earned the title Tennessee Tailor because of his work as a tailor's apprentice and then as the proprietor of his own tailor shop. He first learned the rudiments of reading from an eccentric customer of one of the tailors to whom he was apprenticed. After he married, he was taught to write by his wife, Eliza, who had had some formal schooling. Johnson rose from poverty to politics and was elected to Congress at the age of thirty-four. In 1864, he became Abraham Lincoln's vice president and ascended to the presidency after Lincoln's assassination in 1865.

Vest tailor-made by the young Johnson, 1839.

Q: **Which president once served as a public executioner?**

A: *Grover Cleveland.* As sheriff of Erie County, New York, from 1871 to 1873, Cleveland personally oversaw the public executions of two men, one convicted of stabbing his mother to death and the other guilty of shooting a man after a saloon altercation. It was not a task he welcomed but he felt it was his responsibility, and he would not delegate it to another. During the election of 1884 Cleveland's detractors called him the Buffalo Hangman, but his supporters thought the experience showed him to be a man of integrity.

Who was the shortest president?

A: *James Madison.* At only five feet four and weighing no more than one hundred pounds with clothes and boots on, Madison did not cut an imposing figure. He was shy and socially awkward, too. But the brilliant man known as the Father of the Constitution had the good fortune to marry Dolley Payne Todd, a warm and vivacious woman who charmed visitors to the White House. Often dressed in feathered turbans and fancy gowns, she was the toast of Washington.

Q: **Which president's nickname was inspired by the life of a football player?**

A: *Ronald Reagan.* The man who would become our fortieth president played the role of ailing football star George Gipp in the film *Knute Rockne, All-American*, which was based on the true story of Notre Dame's legendary coach and his star player. In a dramatic scene, Rockne rallies his team by reminding them of Gipp's dying request: "Tell them to go out there with all they've got and win just one for the Gipper." That line lent itself well to Reagan's campaign, in which supporters cried, "Win one for the Gipper!"

Q: **Which president was a successful boxer in college?**

A: *Theodore Roosevelt.* At Harvard, Roosevelt made a name for himself in the ring. He is also remembered for an extraordinary act of sportsmanship. During one bout, his opponent—C. S. Hanks—bloodied Roosevelt's nose after the bell had rung. The crowd booed but Roosevelt silenced them, explaining that Hanks had not heard the bell. Then he walked over and shook Hanks's hand, prompting the spectators to burst into cheers. Roosevelt continued to box in the White House. In one sparring match in the White House gym, he suffered a bad hit, which resulted in a detached retina and cost him the sight in one eye.

Q: Which president cut apart copies of the New Testament to create his own book?

A: *Thomas Jefferson.* Jefferson's personal view of religion can be glimpsed in his cut-and-paste version of the four gospels of the New Testament, edited to form a chronological narrative of Jesus's life, parables, and moral teaching. A project that began when Jefferson was president, the volume was not finished until 1820 when he was seventy-seven. Titled *The Life and Morals of Jesus of Nazareth,* the English text is presented alongside translations in French, Greek, and Latin. The original well-worn red book now resides at the Smithsonian's National Museum of American History.

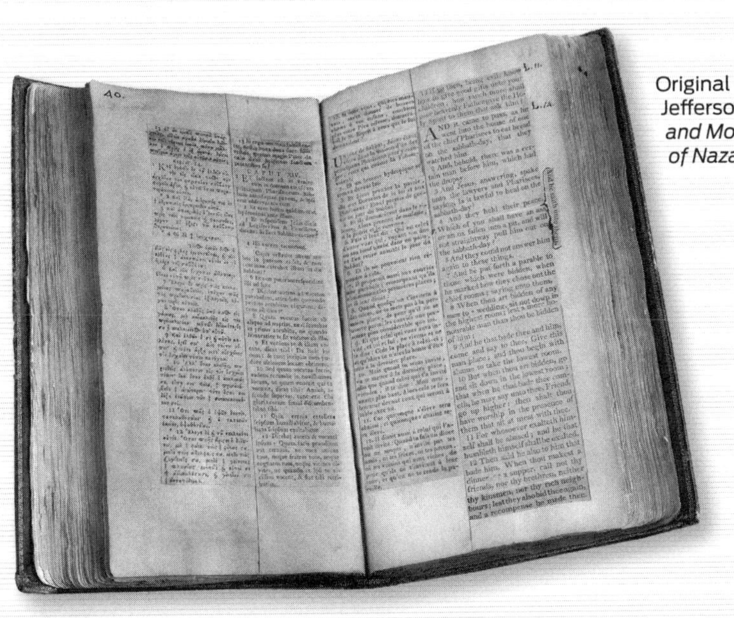

Original copy of Jefferson's *The Life and Morals of Jesus of Nazareth,* 1820.

Q: **Who was the first president of the baby-boom generation?**

A: *Bill Clinton.* Clinton was born on August 19, 1946, in Hope, Arkansas. The baby-boom generation spans birthdates from 1946 to 1964. It refers to an era just after World War II when peace and growth led to a dramatic rise in the birth rate. It also describes a generation of people who lived through a time of upheaval and cultural change, including John F. Kennedy's inauguration and assassination, Woodstock, and the Vietnam War.

Q: **Who were the only two presidents to have signed the Declaration of Independence?**

A: *John Adams and Thomas Jefferson.* Adams was a Massachusetts delegate to the Continental Congress from 1774 to 1777 and served on the committee that drafted the Declaration of Independence. The full responsibility for writing the document fell to Jefferson, a young delegate from Virginia who was known for his eloquent prose. Of the fifty-six delegates to sign the Declaration, only these two men became presidents of the United States.

Q: Who was the youngest president ever elected?

A: *John F. Kennedy.* Although Theodore Roosevelt was the youngest to serve as president—he was only forty-two years old when McKinley's assassination put him in the national driver's seat—Kennedy was the youngest man to be elected by the voters. He was forty-three years old, and his youth and charisma came shining through, particularly on the emerging medium of television, which was gaining popularity in the early 1960s.

Souvenir button from Kennedy's inauguration, January 1961.

Q: **Which president was called the Old Tycoon by his staff?**

A: *Abraham Lincoln.* White House aides affectionately called Lincoln the Old Tycoon, a spin on the Japanese word "taikun," which was a title used for the shoguns (military rulers) of Japan. It was probably the first time the Japanese term was used in America, and it became part of the lexicon, being employed generally to describe businessmen of great wealth and power.

Q: **Which president donated his childhood collection to the Smithsonian?**

A: *Theodore Roosevelt.* Roosevelt was only in his twenties when he offered the National Museum (now the National Museum of Natural History) his childhood natural history cabinet, which he had begun at the age of nine and playfully called the Roosevelt Museum of Natural History. The collection featured insects and nearly 250 carefully labeled specimens of birds and mammals, including a number of Egyptian birds he had collected in the Nile Valley at the age of fourteen. The museum accepted these donations and Roosevelt's continued patronage, even after he became president.

Chapter 2

Stumping: From Front Porch To Facebook

POLITICAL CAMPAIGNS

"I will not make age an issue in this campaign. I am not going to exploit, for political purposes, my opponent's youth and inexperience."

—Ronald Reagan,
in a debate with Walter Mondale, 1984 campaign

Q: **Who was the first presidential candidate to campaign in all fifty states?**

A: *Richard Nixon.* Nixon literally wore himself out in the 1960 campaign, stumping in all fifty states. He banged his knee on a car door in Greensboro, North Carolina, which led to an infection that kept him hospitalized and off the campaign trail for two critical weeks. His opponent, John F. Kennedy, used a different strategy in his campaign, targeting the states with the most electoral votes and offering the visionary message, Leadership for the Sixties. Despite his tireless efforts, Nixon narrowly lost the popular vote.

Nixon presidential campaign button, 1960.

Q: During whose presidential campaign were photographic portraits of the candidates first distributed?

A: *Abraham Lincoln's.* It wasn't until Lincoln's 1860 campaign that mass-produced photographic prints were available for use on campaign buttons and other memorabilia. This was made possible by a new photographic technology: the tintype or ferrotype process. For the first time, voters from all parts of the United States could actually see what a candidate looked like. The 1860 buttons for Lincoln show a clean-shaven candidate, as opposed to his 1864 re-election buttons, on which he sports his famous beard.

Lincoln campaign medallion showing a clean-shaven candidate, 1860.

Wax cylinders used for recording presidential speeches, 1908.

Q: Which presidential candidates made the first sound recordings of campaign speeches?

A: *William Howard Taft and William Jennings Bryan.* The 1908 race between Taft and Bryan marked the first campaign in which voters did not have to travel to hear their candidate; thanks to advances in recording technology, they could listen in their own neighborhoods. Thomas Edison's wax cylinder recordings were mass-produced starting in the early twentieth century, making them more widely available and more reasonably priced. Local theaters capitalized on the use of recordings, providing a venue for those wanting to listen to the "real live" voices of the candidates.

Q:

Who was Old Hickory?

A:

Andrew Jackson. After his defeat of the British in the Battle of New Orleans during the War of 1812, General Jackson earned the nickname Old Hickory. Jackson had been ordered to march his Tennessee troops to Natchez, Mississippi, but when he arrived he was told to disband his men because they were not needed. Jackson refused and marched them back to Tennessee. Because of his strict discipline on that march, his men said he was tough as hickory. Jackson exploited this nickname in his 1828 political campaign, using the image of a hickory tree on leaflets, broadsides, and banners.

Q:

Who was Young Hickory?

A:

James Polk. Although he was a dark-horse candidate for president in the election of 1844, Polk managed to steal the race from Henry Clay. Polk's support for the annexation of Texas, which would come into the Union as a slave state, won him the Southern vote, but he received his share of abuse from the press during the campaign. As a protegé and loyal supporter of Andrew Jackson, popularly known as Old Hickory, Polk was given the nickname Young Hickory.

Q: Which former president was so unhappy with his successor that he formed an alternate party and became its nominee for president?

A: *Theodore Roosevelt.* After leaving the presidency, the energetic Roosevelt traveled to Europe and Africa. On returning home, however, the former president could not sit still. Unhappy with the administration of his successor, William Howard Taft, Roosevelt formed the Progressive Party, also known as the Bull Moose Party because of its moose mascot. Roosevelt's entry into the 1912 presidential race divided Republicans between him and the sitting president, ultimately handing the victory to Democrat Woodrow Wilson.

Bull Moose Party pennant for Roosevelt and Hiram Johnson, 1912.

Q: Who was the first president to have his election take place on the same day throughout the nation?

A: *Zachary Taylor.* The election of 1848, in which Old Rough and Ready triumphed over Lewis Cass, was the first time that voting for president and vice president took place nationwide on the same day: November 7. The only state that did not participate was South Carolina, which left the selection of electors to its legislature. Taylor captured 163 of 290 electoral votes.

Q: Who was the first African American to win nomination as the candidate of one of the two major parties?

A: *Barack Obama.* Obama successfully clinched the nomination in 2008. Other African Americans who aspired to win their party's nomination include: Congresswoman Shirley Chisholm, who sought the Democratic nomination in 1972; Jesse Jackson, who campaigned for the Democratic nomination twice, in 1984 and 1988; Alan Keyes, a Republican, in 1996 and 2000; Senator Carol Moseley Braun, a Democrat, in 2004; activist Al Sharpton, who campaigned for the Democratic nomination in 2004; and Herman Cain, who sought the Republican nomination in 2012.

Q: Which first lady was her husband's unofficial campaign manager?

A: *Florence Harding.* Prior to his entering politics, Mrs. Harding worked with her husband when he was the editor of the *Marion Star* newspaper. As business manager for the paper, she virtually ran the operation. Mrs. Harding later participated actively in Harding's 1920 presidential campaign. She once said, "I know what's best for the president. I put him in the White House."

Mrs. Harding pinning a flower on actor Al Jolson's lapel, 1920 campaign.

Q: Who was the first "log cabin" candidate?

A: *William Henry Harrison.* Ironically, Harrison was born on a country estate, not in a log cabin, but neither his supporters nor detractors were sticklers for detail. Harrison became the "log cabin and hard cider" candidate after *The Baltimore Republican* newspaper blasted him for his backwoods, frontier manner: "Give him a barrel of hard cider and settle a pension of $2,000 a year on him, and my word for it, he will sit the remainder of his days in his log cabin by the side of a sea-coal fire and study moral philosophy." Harrison's Whig party used this depiction to their advantage, holding log cabin campaign rallies at which hard cider was served.

Model log cabin carried in pro-Harrison parades, 1840 campaign.

Q: During whose campaign was the modern political button patented?

A: *William McKinley.* The Whitehead and Hoag Company patented the campaign button in 1896. It was made of four layered pieces: first, a disk of metal; then a printed image with a slogan or photo of the candidate on it; third, a thin piece of see-through celluloid on top of that; and finally a small metal pin attached on the reverse by a machine that pressed all four components into a single button. The buttons for McKinley and his opponent, William Jennings Bryan, were enormously popular.

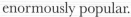

McKinley and Bryan campaign buttons, 1896.

Q: Which first lady made her own Whistle Stop Campaign?

A: *Lady Bird Johnson.* During her husband's 1964 presidential campaign, Lady Bird made a solo train trip through the South to urge voters to cast their ballots for LBJ. Called the *Lady Bird Special*, the train made stops between Virginia and Louisiana so Mrs. Johnson could greet supporters and address the public.

Model of Lady Bird Johnson's train, with button and map of route, 1964.

Q: Which candidates participated in the first televised debates?

A: *John F. Kennedy and Richard Nixon.* Kennedy and Nixon faced each other on camera for the first time on September 26, 1960, before a TV audience of 70 million. Nixon, looking pale and haggard from the demanding campaign, mopped his brow under the hot studio lights and appeared unsettled and defensive. The youthful Kennedy seemed tanned, prepared, and relaxed. While both candidates were well versed on the issues, it was Kennedy's physical appeal that wooed voters. The television camera forever changed the landscape of political elections.

Chairs used by Nixon and Kennedy during television debates, 1960.

Q: **Which president had his election to the presidency literally decided by one man?**

A: *Thomas Jefferson.* Jefferson's election was due to a bold act by Congressman James Bayard of Delaware. In the race of 1800, due to a quirk in the Constitution that was later rectified, Jefferson and his running mate, Aaron Burr, the two candidates of the Democratic-Republican Party, were tied in the Electoral College after defeating the Federalist ticket headed by incumbent John Adams. The election was therefore sent to the House of Representatives for a state-by-state vote. After thirty-five ballots, there was no clear winner. Bayard decided to abstain on the thirty-sixth ballot, and he convinced other Federalists to follow suit, thereby breaking the deadlock. Thus he secured Jefferson's and his own place in history.

Q: **Which president is associated with the phrase "keep the ball rolling"?**

A: *William Henry Harrison.* In one of the great campaign publicity stunts of presidential elections, Harrison supporters rolled a ten-foot tin and paper ball, plastered with campaign slogans, from Kentucky to Baltimore. This activity gave rise to the song lyrics: "What has caused this great commotion, motion, motion/ Our country through?/ It is the ball a-rolling on, on/ For Tippecanoe and Tyler, too."

Q: Who was the only president elected to more than two terms?

A: *Franklin D. Roosevelt.* The Twenty-second Amendment, setting a two-term limit for presidents, was enacted *after* Roosevelt was elected to office for the fourth time. It formalized a tradition started by George Washington, who refused to run for a third term in 1796. The amendment, ratified in 1951, states: "No person shall be elected to the office of the President more than twice, and no person who has held the office of President, or acted as President, for more than two years of a term to which some other person was elected President shall be elected to the office of the President more than once."

Pro- and anti-third-term buttons from 1940 election.

Q: **Who was the only president to be elected to two non-consecutive terms in office?**

A: *Grover Cleveland.* Cleveland won the 1884 election, but was ousted in the 1888 contest by Benjamin Harrison. Four years later, in 1892, the man known as Old Veto was back. Cleveland's second term was plagued by an economic crisis, referred to as the Panic of 1893, and labor unrest. He failed to win back his party's confidence for a third nomination.

Q: **Who was the first presidential candidate to have news of his nomination telegraphed?**

A: *James Polk.* News of Polk's nomination in May 1844 was telegraphed from Baltimore (the site of the convention) to Washington, D.C. This was the first use of the newly invented telegraph to disseminate such information. However, back in Tennessee, Polk himself did not learn of his nomination until several days later.

Q: **How many presidential candidates lost the popular vote but obtained the highest office in the U.S.?**

A: *Four: John Quincy Adams, Rutherford B. Hayes, Benjamin Harrison, and George W. Bush.* Four candidates won the popular vote but lost the presidency: Andrew Jackson to Adams (1824); Samuel Tilden to Hayes (1876); Grover Cleveland to Harrison (1888); and Al Gore to Bush (2000).

Q: Which president was elected only after a legal battle that went to the Supreme Court?

A: *George W. Bush*. In the 2000 election between Bush and Al Gore, the results from forty-nine states failed to produce the 270 electoral votes needed for either candidate to declare victory, leaving Florida's voters to decide who would get that state's twenty-five electoral votes and win the national election. Although Bush initially seemed to have the lead in Florida, the popular vote was so close that Gore demanded a recount. There were also reports of voting irregularities (poorly designed ballots that confused voters, "hanging chads" on punch cards that made it difficult to divine the voters' intent), which created more havoc. Ultimately, it was up to the Supreme Court to decide if a recount should go forward. Weeks later, the court ruled a statewide recount unconstitutional, concluding that it would violate the equal protection clause of the Fourteenth Amendment, and Bush was declared the winner.

Controversial Florida ballot, 2000 election.

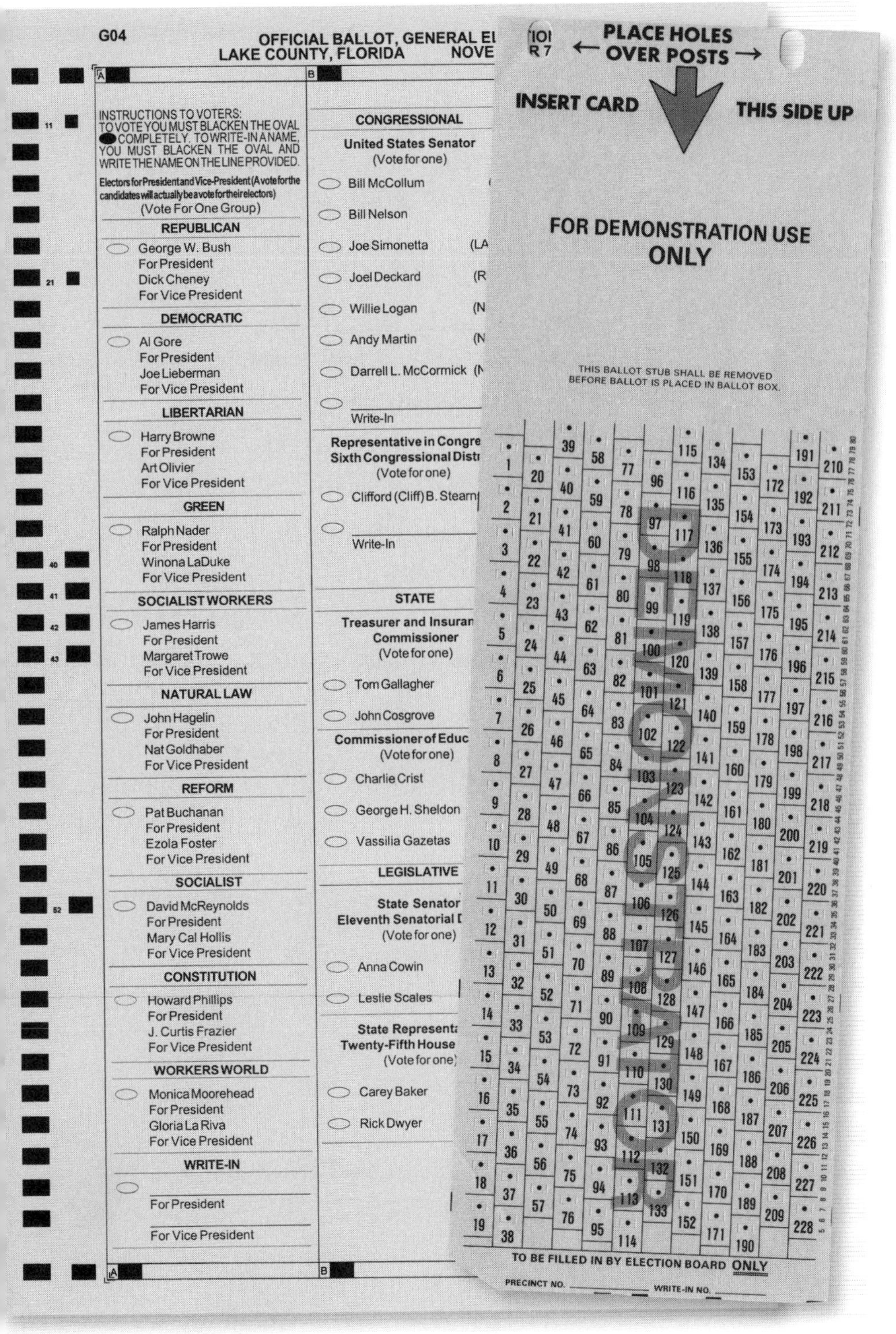

G04

OFFICIAL BALLOT, GENERAL EL... ...TION
LAKE COUNTY, FLORIDA NOVE... ...R 7

A

INSTRUCTIONS TO VOTERS:
TO VOTE YOU MUST BLACKEN THE OVAL COMPLETELY. TO WRITE-IN A NAME, YOU MUST BLACKEN THE OVAL AND WRITE THE NAME ON THE LINE PROVIDED.

Electors for President and Vice-President (A vote for the candidates will actually be a vote for their electors)
(Vote For One Group)

REPUBLICAN
George W. Bush For President
Dick Cheney For Vice President

DEMOCRATIC
Al Gore For President
Joe Lieberman For Vice President

LIBERTARIAN
Harry Browne For President
Art Olivier For Vice President

GREEN
Ralph Nader For President
Winona LaDuke For Vice President

SOCIALIST WORKERS
James Harris For President
Margaret Trowe For Vice President

NATURAL LAW
John Hagelin For President
Nat Goldhaber For Vice President

REFORM
Pat Buchanan For President
Ezola Foster For Vice President

SOCIALIST
David McReynolds For President
Mary Cal Hollis For Vice President

CONSTITUTION
Howard Phillips For President
J. Curtis Frazier For Vice President

WORKERS WORLD
Monica Moorehead For President
Gloria La Riva For Vice President

WRITE-IN
For President
For Vice President

B

CONGRESSIONAL

United States Senator
(Vote for one)
Bill McCollum
Bill Nelson
Joe Simonetta (LA
Joel Deckard (R
Willie Logan (N
Andy Martin (N
Darrell L. McCormick (N
Write-In

Representative in Congre...
Sixth Congressional Distr...
(Vote for one)
Clifford (Cliff) B. Stearn...
Write-In

STATE

Treasurer and Insuran...
Commissioner
(Vote for one)
Tom Gallagher
John Cosgrove

Commissioner of Educ...
(Vote for one)
Charlie Crist
George H. Sheldon
Vassilia Gazetas

LEGISLATIVE

State Senator
Eleventh Senatorial D...
(Vote for one)
Anna Cowin
Leslie Scales

State Representa...
Twenty-Fifth House...
(Vote for one)
Carey Baker
Rick Dwyer

← PLACE HOLES OVER POSTS →

INSERT CARD THIS SIDE UP

FOR DEMONSTRATION USE ONLY

THIS BALLOT STUB SHALL BE REMOVED BEFORE BALLOT IS PLACED IN BALLOT BOX.

DEMONSTRATION

TO BE FILLED IN BY ELECTION BOARD ONLY

PRECINCT NO. ________ WRITE-IN NO. ________

Q: Which war hero was solicited by both the Democratic and Republican parties to run for president?

A: *Dwight Eisenhower.* The supreme commander of the Allied Expeditionary Forces in World War II was one of the most esteemed figures in America after victory in 1945. Both parties saw him as a winner and tried to woo him into the presidential race in 1948, but he declined and voted Republican—for Dewey. The pressure on him to run mounted again in 1952, and this time he went with the Republicans, winning the nomination on the first ballot.

Campaign button with Eisenhower's catchy slogan, 1952.

Q: Who was Old Tippecanoe?

A: *William Henry Harrison.* In 1811, while serving as governor of the Indiana Territory, Harrison battled against Indian chief Tecumseh and his Shawnee warriors in the brutal Battle of Tippecanoe. Harrison's forces defeated the Indians, and soon after he acquired the nickname Old Tippecanoe. When Harrison teamed up with vice presidential candidate John Tyler in 1840, the rallying cry for the Whigs became "Tippecanoe and Tyler, too!"

Harrison ribbon lauding the hero of Tippecanoe, 1840.

Q: Which presidential candidates participated in the first election between two parties?

A: *John Adams and Thomas Jefferson.* Once George Washington retired, his would-be successors bared their fangs and released their venom. In the election of 1796, the Federalists, led by John Adams, advocated a strong central government. The Democratic-Republicans, led by Jefferson, favored states rights. The battle grew ugly and personal. Adams ultimately prevailed. The political parties endured, and this first use of negative campaigning to influence voters became an American tradition.

Banner commemorating Jefferson's victory in 1800 reads, "T Jefferson President of the United States/ John Adams is no more."

Q: Who was the first presidential candidate to appear on MTV?

A: *Bill Clinton.* In 1992, Democratic candidate Clinton visited the music video channel MTV to tape a special program aimed at young voters called *Choose or Lose*. During the filming, audience members had an opportunity to ask Clinton questions, some of them fairly direct. "If you had it to do over again, would you inhale?" one youthful questioner asked in reference to Clinton's prior marijuana use. Clinton managed to finesse the response and went on to win the election, crediting MTV with bringing votes to the ticket of Clinton and Al Gore.

Sax-player Clinton as the epitome of cool on a campaign pin, 1992.

Q: Who was the only president never actually elected to either the office of president or vice president?

A: *Gerald Ford.* The thirty-eighth president never expected to work in the Oval Office. His first promotion came when Richard Nixon's vice president, Spiro Agnew, resigned amid a bribery scandal in 1973. Nixon chose Ford to take Agnew's place. A year later, Nixon was in hot water for conducting a cover-up of the Watergate scandal. He resigned from the presidency in disgrace, leaving Ford to take over the reins of government.

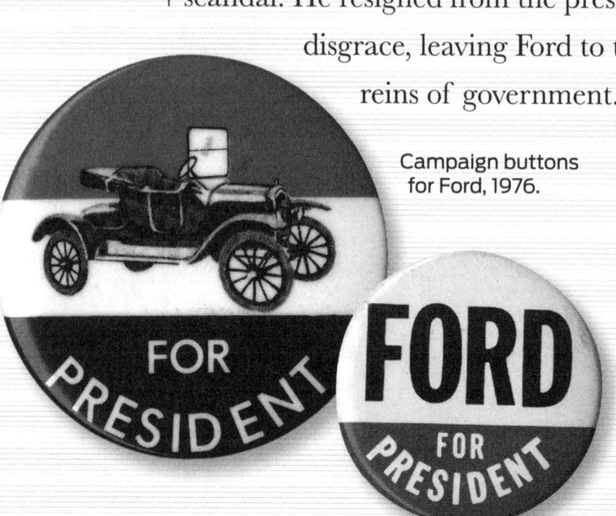

Campaign buttons for Ford, 1976.

Q: Who is the only president to have been elected by unanimous electoral vote?

A: *George Washington.* No one can top Washington's record. In his first election, he got all sixty-nine electoral votes from the ten states that cast them. Then the Father of Our Country, who still enjoyed preeminent status as a hero of the Revolutionary War, did it again in 1792, winning all 132 electoral votes and all fifteen states. Washington had an advantage over his successors in that there was not yet a two-party system in America, so he faced little opposition.

Q: Who was the first president to effectively use social media in his campaign?

A: *Barack Obama.* In his successful 2008 presidential campaign, Obama employed Facebook, Twitter, Flickr, LinkedIn, YouTube, and his own site, barackobama.com, to deliver his message and encourage feedback from voters. Campaign strategists used social media to keep the buzz about their candidate alive by constantly updating blogs, posting new photographs, airing videos of Obama's speeches, and organizing rallies across America. Supporters were encouraged to post their own views and photos as well, allowing the grassroots effort to swell and campaign donations from individuals to multiply.

Q: Which presidential campaign used surplus military material to promote its candidate?

A: *Dwight Eisenhower's.* The 1956 Eisenhower Bandwagon campaign employed jeeps, barrage balloons (large tethered balloons used to defend against low-level aircraft attack), and other material associated with the heroic five-star general, to promote the candidate. Painted with the slogans "I like Ike," or simply "Ike," in red and white, the items could not fail to impress citizens, who saw the pageantry of war turned into a parade of peace. Accompanying the campaign caravan as it made its way around the country were festive troops—local girls—wearing Ike dresses and carrying Ike parasols.

Military barrage balloon used in Eisenhower campaign, 1956.

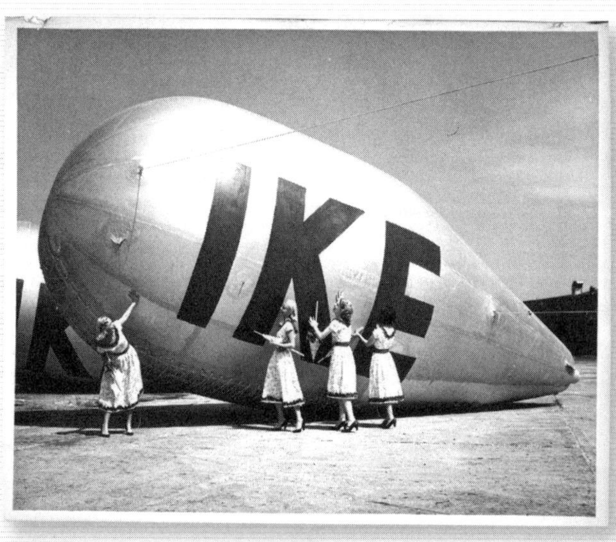

Chapter 3

The Pledge and the Parties

INAUGURATIONS AND INAUGURAL BALLS

"And so, my fellow Americans: ask not what your country can do for you; ask what you can do for your country."

—*John F. Kennedy*, *inaugural address, January 20, 1961*

Q: Which president's inaugural speech may have killed him?

A: *William Henry Harrison.* Harrison recited 8,445 words in a speech that may have literally cost him his life. It was a chilly March day in the capital city and the president stood outside without hat, gloves, or coat. Later, he was out walking and got caught in a downpour. Soon he came down with a cold that turned into pneumonia. His last words were, "I wish you to understand the true principles of government. I wish them carried out. I ask nothing more." Recent analysis by medical experts has cast doubt on this popular version of Harrison's death, with many commentators questioning whether a cold contracted on March 4 could lead to death a full month later. Records seem to indicate that Harrison contracted a second cold on March 28, which quickly turned into pneumonia and led to his death on April 4. Certainly Harrison's reckless disregard for the weather contributed to his demise.

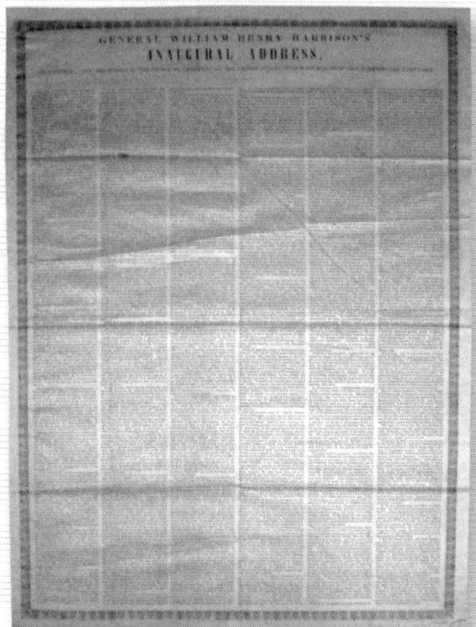
GENERAL WILLIAM HENRY HARRISON'S
INAUGURAL ADDRESS.

Printed copy of Harrison's lengthy inaugural address, 1841.

Q: **Who held the first official inaugural ball?**

A: *James Madison.* Although there was a ball in 1789 to honor the election of George Washington, the first official inaugural ball did not occur until 1809, when Madison took office. Madison was sworn in at the U.S. Capitol. That evening his wife, Dolley Madison, hosted a gala at Long's Hotel. The price of admission was four dollars per ticket. Four hundred tickets were sold, and so began a Washington tradition. Today the Presidential Inaugural Committee plans all the official inaugural balls.

Q: **Who was the only president to use the words "I affirm" as he took the oath of office rather than "I swear"?**

A: *Franklin Pierce.* At his swearing-in on March 4, 1853, Pierce opted for religious reasons to use the words "I affirm," a choice offered by the Constitution. He was also the first president to recite his inaugural speech (3,329 words) from memory, without any notes.

Q: **Which inaugural parades showcased the following floats?**

A. log cabin; B. hot air balloon; C. Buffalo Bill; D. PT boat; E. ranch.

A: *A. William Henry Harrison (1841); B. James Buchanan (1857); C. Benjamin Harrison (1889); D. John F. Kennedy (1961); E. Lyndon Johnson (1965).* The custom of having inaugural parades on Pennsylvania Avenue following the presidential address began in 1889. Before that time, parades started at the White House and escorted the president to the Capitol. Twentieth-century parades were marked by lavish floats and spectacular marching bands. Theodore Roosevelt's inaugural parade was especially memorable, including coal miners complete with headlamps, African American troops of the Ninth Cavalry, and TR's own Rough Riders.

Q: **Who was the only president sworn in by a woman?**

Lyndon Johnson. Johnson was sworn in by U.S. District Court Judge Sarah T. Hughes on Air Force One, just hours after President John F. Kennedy was assassinated in Dallas, Texas, on November 22, 1963. The plane carried the new president and the slain former president's body back to Washington, D.C.

Q: Who was the only first lady to attend the inaugural ball without her husband?

A: *Eleanor Roosevelt.* After giving his inaugural address in 1933 to a country ravaged by the Great Depression, FDR announced that the first couple would not be attending the inaugural ball planned for that evening. But on hearing that scores were cancelling their reservations for the event, which was a charity fundraiser, Mrs. Roosevelt announced that she would go alone—and in so doing became the first first lady to attend an inaugural ball without the president.

Slate-blue silk crepe evening gown, worn by Mrs. Roosevelt to the inaugural ball in 1933.

Q: **Who was the first president to take the oath in Washington, D.C.?**

A: *Thomas Jefferson.* After one of the most contentious elections in history, Jefferson took the oath on March 4, 1801, in the unfinished Capitol building in Washington, D.C. According to a report in the *Alexandria Times*, Jefferson wore the clothes "of a plain citizen without any distinct badge of office," rather than donning an elegant suit or uniform. Instead of taking a coach, he walked to the packed Senate chamber and delivered his speech in a barely audible voice before taking the oath administered by Chief Justice John Marshall at the clerk's desk. Jefferson's second inauguration in 1805 featured the first inaugural parade.

Q: **Which president was the first to be sworn in on live television?**

A: *Harry Truman.* Coverage of Truman's inaugural on live television made it the most widely viewed single event of its time. An estimated ten million Americans saw the swearing-in of the thirty-third president. Truman's 1949 inaugural was full of firsts. It marked the debut of the current presidential seal of the United States; it was the first openly racially integrated inaugural in modern times; and it was the most expensive and elaborate inauguration to that date (including grandstand, gala, and fireworks).

Q: Which president hosted the first inaugural ball to be fully illuminated by electric lights?

A: *William McKinley.* In 1901, the great hall of Washington's Pension Building sparkled with thousands of electric lights for McKinley's second inaugural ball. There were twelve thousand guests in attendance. Electricity was not the only novelty at this festive event. Rough Rider hats, celebrating Theodore Roosevelt, McKinley's new vice president, were the must-have souvenirs of the twenty-ninth inauguration.

The great hall of the Pension Building illuminated for McKinley's ball, 1901.

Q: **Who was the first president to invite a poet to read at his inauguration?**

A: *John F. Kennedy*. Kennedy invited Robert Frost to read at the occasion of his inaugural. The eighty-six-year-old poet from New England had written a special work called "Dedication" specifically for the event. However, the glare from the sun made it difficult for Frost to see his text. Instead, he recited "The Gift Outright" from memory. Afterward, he sent a handwritten copy of the poem to the Smithsonian.

Frost's handwritten copy of "The Gift Outright," 1961.

The Gift Outright

The land was ours before we were the land's
She was our land more than a hundred years
Before we were her people. She was ours
In Massachusetts in Virginia
But we were England's, still colonials,
Possessing what we still were unpossessed by,
Possessed by what we now no more possessed.
Something we were withholding made us weak
Until we found out that it was ourselves
We were withholding from our land of living
And forthwith found salvation in surrender.
Such as we were we gave ourselves outright
(The deed of gift was many deeds of war)
To the land vaguely realizing westward,
But still unstoried artless unenhanced
Such as she was such as she would become

Robert Frost

For the Inauguration
Of John F. Kennedy.

To the Smithsonian

1961

Q: Who was sworn in using his nickname instead of his given name?

A: *Jimmy Carter.* In keeping with his unpretentious style, Carter used "Jimmy" instead of "James Earl" at his swearing-in. His inauguration departed from tradition in another way as well. After his speech, he, his wife, Rosalynn, and, for some of the way, their daughter, Amy, walked hand-in-hand from the Capitol to the White House. The forty-minute walk in place of the traditional limousine ride was full of symbolism: here was a president who was in touch with the American people.

Q: Which president was forced to borrow a bible for his first inaugural?

A: *George Washington.* Maybe it was pre-inaugural jitters, or just the fact that there was no precedent for the ceremony, but someone forgot to bring a bible for the swearing-in of America's first president in New York City. In fact, no one thought of it until the last minute, so Jacob Morton, a parade marshal and master of St. John's Masonic Lodge No. 1, retrieved the lodge's 1767 edition of the King James Bible and gave it to Robert R. Livingston, New York state chancellor and presiding grand master of Masons in New York, who administered the oath of office to Washington.

Q: Which president's inaugural party forced him to flee the White House?

A: *Andrew Jackson.* After his inaugural, Jackson generously invited ordinary Americans to the Executive Mansion to celebrate. Perhaps he didn't count on the response. As many as twenty thousand callers turned up, ready to party. They caused such a ruckus that Jackson was forced to flee to a nearby hotel. Jackson's aides stayed behind and tried to lure souvenir seekers and rabble-rousers out of the building by filling washtubs with orange juice and whiskey and placing them on the White House lawn.

Q: Which president was the first to have his inauguration broadcast by radio?

A: *Calvin Coolidge.* How ironic that Silent Cal was the first president to have his inaugural broadcast by radio. It was carried on twenty-one stations to between fifteen and twenty-five million people. Coolidge used the new medium to connect with Americans. In his first year in office, he spoke an average of nine thousand words per month over radio.

Q: Who was the first first lady to donate her inaugural gown to the Smithsonian?

A: *Helen "Nellie" Taft.* Taft's 1909 inaugural ball gown, by the Frances Smith Company, now in the collections of the National Museum of American History, is made of white silk chiffon with floral embroideries in metallic thread and trimmed with rhinestones and beads. Taft established a precedent of having first ladies donate the gowns they wore to the ball. The first ladies' inaugural gowns are among the most popular exhibits at the Smithsonian.

Helen Taft's bejeweled inaugural gown, 1901.

Q: Who was the first president to ride to his inaugural in a car instead of a carriage?

A: *Warren Harding.* Harding was driven in a car—not the traditional carriage—to his 1921 inauguration. He also returned to the White House in a car, riding with Mrs. Harding in a Packer Twin Six up Pennsylvania Avenue during the inaugural parade. The Harding inaugural was also the first at which loudspeakers were used.

Q: Which three presidents had to re-take the oath of office?

A: *Chester Arthur, Calvin Coolidge, and Barack Obama.* Arthur, who served from 1881 to 1885, was sworn in by a justice of the New York State Supreme Court in a private ceremony following the assassination of President James Garfield. Arthur was sworn in a second time by the chief justice of the U.S. Supreme Court two days later at the Capitol. Coolidge took the oath of office at his father's Vermont home following the death of President Warren Harding. Coolidge's father was a notary public and administered the oath. Concerns about the jurisdiction of Coolidge's father led to Coolidge taking a second oath later in Washington, D.C. At his swearing-in on January 20, 2009, Obama improperly recited the oath because he was repeating after Chief Justice John Roberts, who transposed the words "faithfully" and "execute." He had to retake the oath the following day.

Q: Which president decided to call his inaugural "balls" inaugural "parties"?

A: *Jimmy Carter.* The word "ball" sounded too elitist to the low-key Southern president. He wanted to connect with people in a more direct way than his predecessors. Tickets to his "inaugural parties" cost only $25 each. His 1977 inauguration also marked the first time there were accommodations for those with disabilities to watch the parade, and the reviewing stand for dignitaries was solar heated.

Ticket for Carter's low-key inaugural "party," 1977.

The Inaugural Party
Nº 13317
Thursday Evening, January 20, 1977
9:00 p.m.
District of Columbia National Guard Armory
2001 East Capitol Street
Admit One
$25.00
District of Columbia
National Guard Armory
Nº 13317

Q: Who was the first president to have more than one official ball on the evening of his inaugural?

A: *Dwight Eisenhower.* Organizers of Eisenhower's 1953 inauguration added a second ball, due to the demand for tickets. The number of balls escalated after that. Four years later, Eisenhower's second inauguration featured four balls. John F. Kennedy attended five in 1961. By the second inaugural of Bill Clinton in 1997, the number of balls had reached an all-time high of fourteen. George W. Bush's inaugural in 2001 saw the number of official balls decline to eight, and his second inaugural in 2005 was celebrated with nine official balls. Barack Obama had ten official balls.

Q: In one year there were three presidents. What was the year and who were they?

A: *1841: Martin Van Buren, William Henry Harrison, and John Tyler.* Eighth president Van Buren completed his term on March 3, 1841. Harrison was inaugurated ninth president the next day but died soon after, on April 4. Vice President Tyler was then sworn in as the nation's tenth president.

Q: Who was the first first lady to ride along with her husband in the parade from the Capitol to the White House after his inauguration?

A: *Helen "Nellie" Taft.* As a child Nellie Herron dreamed of being first lady. Perhaps that's why, when her wish came true in 1909, the independent Taft broke with tradition and rode to the White House beside the newly inaugurated president in an open carriage. Previous first ladies had dutifully followed behind their husbands in a separate vehicle.

William and Nellie Taft's open carriage in the inaugural parade, 1909.

Q: Who was the first president to be inaugurated in January instead of March?

A: *Franklin D. Roosevelt.* On January 20, 1937, Roosevelt became the first president sworn into office in January, per the Twentieth Amendment to the Constitution. Prior to that time, all inaugurals were in early March. In the eighteenth century, when the March date was established, it took longer to complete the transfer of power. Votes needed to be tallied by hand and the members of the Electoral College had to send their ballots to Washington. In the twentieth century, modern communication made the process easier, and a delay only gave the outgoing administration more time to create havoc for its successor.

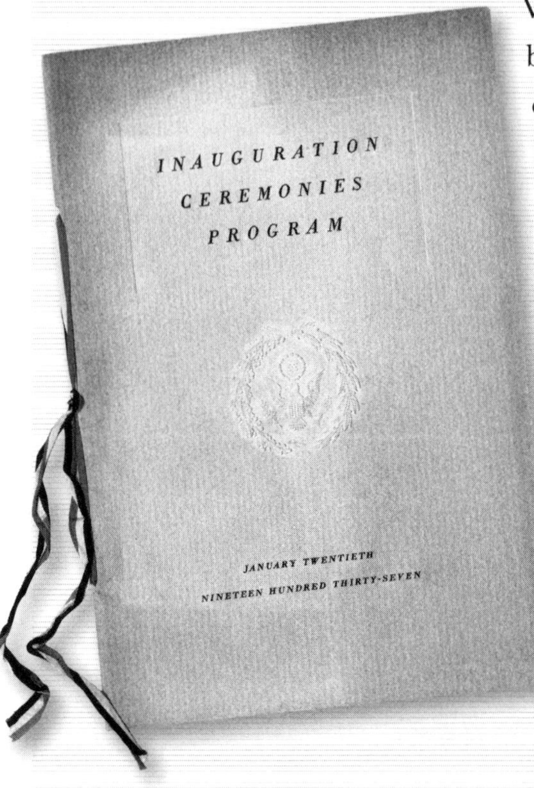

INAUGURATION
CEREMONIES
PROGRAM
JANUARY TWENTIETH
NINETEEN HUNDRED THIRTY-SEVEN

Program for Roosevelt's January inaugural, 1937.

Q: **Which president was sworn in by a former president?**

A: *Calvin Coolidge.* On March 4, 1925, for the first time in American history, a former president, Chief Justice William Howard Taft, officiated at the inaugural ceremony. Taft had been the twenty-seventh president. Warren Harding appointed him to the Supreme Court in 1921. Some fifteen to twenty-five million people tuned in by radio to hear Coolidge take the oath. Sadly, the festivities were somber, as the Coolidges were still mourning the death of their teenage son the previous July.

Q: **Who traveled undercover to Washington for his inaugural?**

A: *Abraham Lincoln.* In 1861, with a country on the brink of war, Lincoln could not afford to take chances. Hearing of a threat to assassinate him en route to his inaugural, he slipped into Washington undetected. Security was stepped up for the event, with policemen stationed in the crowd and sharpshooters in position on Pennsylvania Avenue rooftops. Still, the president rode up to the Capitol in an open carriage and arrived for the swearing-in unharmed.

Q: Who had six Native American chiefs in his inaugural parade?

A: *Theodore Roosevelt.* Among the thirty-five thousand participants in Roosevelt's 1905 inaugural parade were chiefs Quanah Parker (Comanche), Buckskin Charlie (Ute), American Horse (Sioux), Little Plume (Blackfeet), Hollow Horn Bear (Sioux), and Geronimo (Apache). While in Washington for the festivities, the chiefs took the opportunity to meet with the president and ask for the return of land confiscated by the U.S. government.

Q: Which president refused to be inaugurated on Sunday, leaving the highest post in the land vacant for a day?

A: *Zachary Taylor.* In March 1849, Taylor refused to take the oath of office on a Sunday due to his religious beliefs. The offices of president and vice president expired at noon on March 4, which meant that, according to the rules of succession at that time, David Rice Atchison, president pro tempore of the Senate, was next in line to the presidency. He always claimed he held the office for a day, but others have pointed out that his Senate term expired on March 4 as well, giving little credence to the existence of an "Atchison administration."

Q: Who was the first first lady to have her inaugural gown on display at the Smithsonian while she was still in the White House?

A:

Mamie Eisenhower. Eisenhower wore a pink peau de soie gown, embroidered with more than 2,000 rhinestones, to the 1953 inaugural balls. Nettie Rosenstein designed the dress. Despite public pressure to release details, Eisenhower waited until the week before the inauguration to reveal descriptions of her sparkling pink gown, along with formal photographs, to the newspapers. She donated the gown to the Smithsonian in 1955.

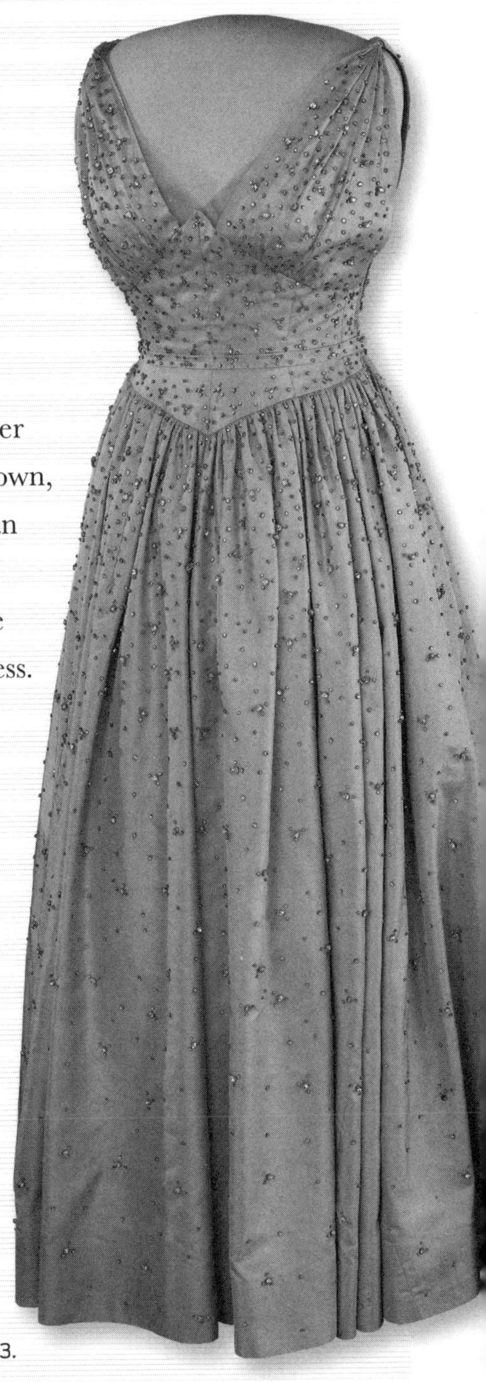

Mamie Eisenhower's pink rhinestone-studded inaugural gown, 1953.

Q: Which president was sworn in by his father?

A: *Calvin Coolidge.* Vice President Coolidge was vacationing in his family's farmhouse in Vermont on the evening of August 2, 1923, when news came of President Warren Harding's death. Coolidge's father, a notary public, administered the oath of office to his son by the light of a kerosene lamp. Although the family bible was at hand, it was not used for the administration of the oath.

Q: Which president gave the shortest inaugural address?

A: *George Washington.* Washington must have felt he had said it all the first time around. His second inaugural speech on March 4, 1793, was only 135 words. He began, "Fellow citizens: I am again called upon by the voice of my country to execute the functions of its Chief Magistrate," and ended, "If it shall be found during my administration of the Government I have in any instance violated willingly or knowingly the injunctions thereof, I may … be subject to the upbraidings of all who are now witnesses of the present solemn ceremony."

Q: Who was the first president to celebrate his inauguration in a Smithsonian building?

A: *James Garfield.* On March 4, 1881, Garfield became the first president to hold an inaugural ball in a Smithsonian building. The festivities were also the first event held in the new Arts and Industries Building (then known as the National Museum Building) before it opened to the public.

Invitation to Garfield's inaugural reception at the National Museum (now the Smithsonian), 1881.

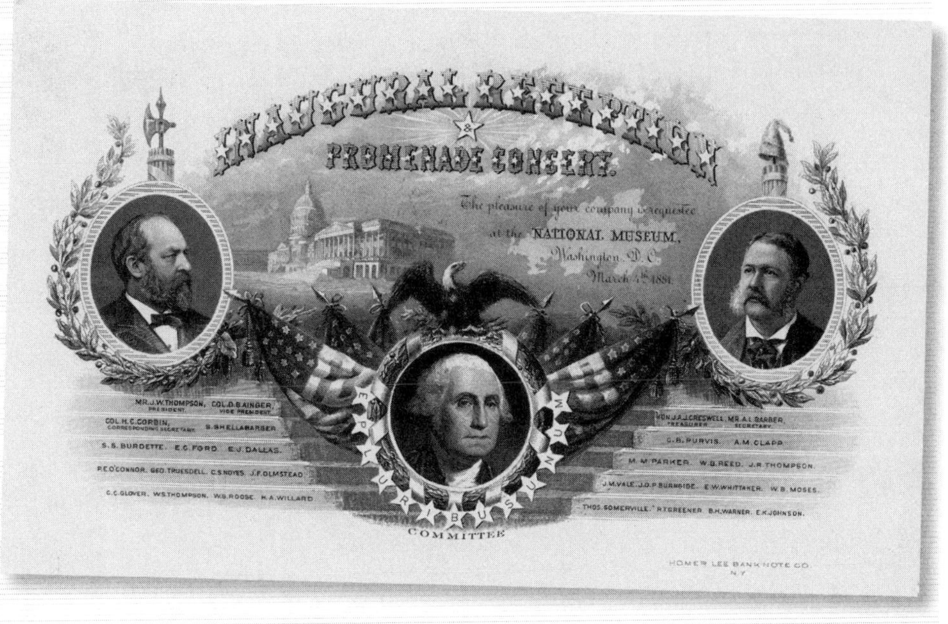

Q: Who was the first president to have his swearing-in broadcast live on the Internet?

A: *Bill Clinton.* Clinton's second inaugural in 1997 was the first time Americans could enjoy the event online. This technological advance was in keeping with Clinton's theme of creating a "bridge to the twenty-first century." In his speech, Clinton declared: "At the dawn of the twenty-first century, a free people must now choose to shape the forces of the Information Age and the global society, to unleash the limitless potential of all our people, and, yes, to form a more perfect union."

Which president wore a ring containing a lock of Lincoln's hair to his inauguration?

A: *Theodore Roosevelt.* Roosevelt wore a ring with a lock of Lincoln's hair in it on March 4, 1905, at his second inauguration. Roosevelt had been a long-time admirer of Lincoln, and as a child had watched Lincoln's funeral procession pass by his house in New York. Roosevelt's admiration for Lincoln was reinforced later, when he met John Hay, who had worked for Lincoln in the White House. Hay and Roosevelt talked about Lincoln often, and Hay gave Roosevelt the ring, knowing that Roosevelt would treasure it.

Chapter 4

Inside the Oval Office

THE PRESIDENT AT WORK—AS CHIEF EXECUTIVE, DIPLOMAT, PARTY LEADER

"My God, this is a hell of a job!"

—*Warren Harding*

Q: Which president nearly doubled the size of the country without consulting Congress?

A: *Thomas Jefferson.* Jefferson made a bold decision on behalf of the country in 1803 when he purchased the Louisiana Territory from France for fifteen million dollars—despite the fact that the Constitution did not explicitly give him the authority to do so. The country was thereby nearly doubled in size. In 1804 Jefferson sent Meriwether Lewis and William Clark to explore the newly acquired lands, chronicling flora and fauna and mapping uncharted areas of the continent.

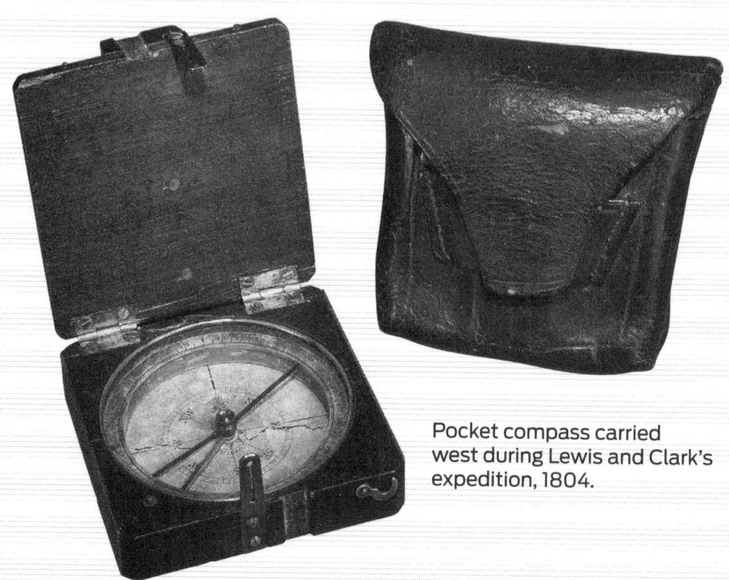

Pocket compass carried west during Lewis and Clark's expedition, 1804.

Q: Which first lady was accused of running the government after the president became ill?

A: *Edith Wilson.* Edith was Woodrow Wilson's second wife. After his first—Ellen—died, Wilson quickly became engaged to and married wealthy widow Edith Galt. When the president suffered a stroke in 1919, he did not relinquish his powers and Edith, in effect, became gatekeeper to the Oval Office, screening his visitors and monitoring all his correspondence. The press criticized her influence on the executive office and called it a "regency."

Q: Which president had a sign on his desk that read, "The buck stops here"?

A: *Harry Truman.* The plainspoken and confident president kept the sign on his desk. It reminded him—and others—that he alone was responsible for the tough decisions of the presidency, for good or ill. Another favorite Truman line was, "If you can't stand the heat, get out of the kitchen." This reflected his personal philosophy about the strength needed to endure in the turbulent and demanding world of politics.

Q: Which president spoke to astronauts on the moon by telephone?

A: *Richard Nixon.* On July 20, 1969, Neil Armstrong became the first man to walk on the surface of the moon, followed by his colleague Buzz Aldrin several minutes later. An estimated six hundred million people watched the moon landing on television. During the moonwalk the astronauts took photographs, gathered soil samples, and raised an American flag. Later they received the first earth-to-moon phone call—what Nixon referred to as "the most historic telephone call ever made from the White House"—as the president offered the astronauts his congratulations on their work.

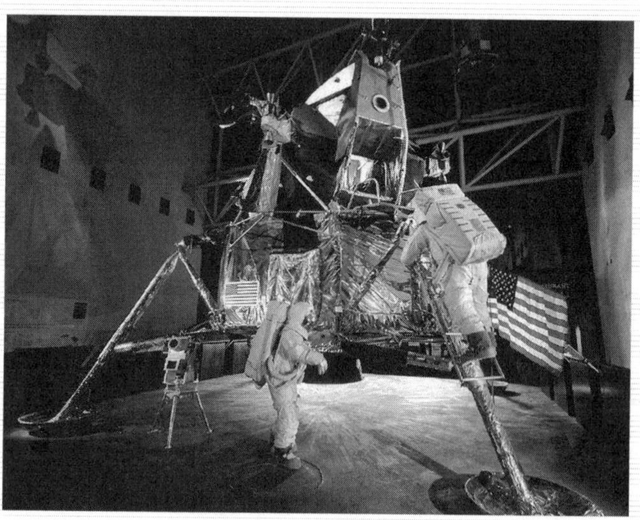

Lunar lander used by astronauts on the first moon walk, July 1969.

Q: Who was the first president to work in the Oval Office?

A: *William Howard Taft.* The Oval Office has been the workplace of the president since Taft first occupied it in late 1909. After his inauguration, Taft held a competition to select an architect to enlarge and make permanent the West Wing's "temporary" executive office. The winning architect was Nathan C. Wyeth of Washington, D.C., who modeled the space after the White House's original oval-shaped Blue Room. FDR would later have the office redesigned (while retaining its oval shape) and moved to its present location on the southeast corner of the White House.

Q: Which president's policies were so strongly criticized by anti-war protesters that he decided not to seek reelection?

A: *Lyndon Johnson.* Anti– Vietnam War protesters, who demanded immediate troop withdrawal from a conflict they thought unjustified, condemned LBJ's policy of "victory with honor." Johnson's decision not to seek reelection was largely determined by his dwindling popularity as a result of this failed foreign policy. The president, who had been *Time* magazine's Man of the Year after his landslide victory in 1964, did not have a clear thumbs-up from his party for the '68 run.

Q: Who was the first president to name a woman to his cabinet?

A: *Franklin D. Roosevelt.* FDR named Frances Perkins as secretary of labor in 1933. The Mount Holyoke College graduate was a trained social worker who had worked in settlement houses in Chicago and Philadelphia. Her efforts on behalf of labor reform took on added urgency after the tragic Triangle Shirtwaist Factory fire in 1911. She served as industrial commissioner under Roosevelt when he was governor of New York. As labor secretary, Perkins established the Labor Standards Bureau and was a principal architect of the Social Security Act.

Bronze statue of Perkins by Max Kalish, 1944.

Q: Who was the first president to visit a foreign country while in office?

A: *Theodore Roosevelt.* The Panama Canal project was important to Roosevelt. He used American might to get the canal built, even sparking a rebellion in Colombia to bring about a treaty that would allow the venture to move forward. In 1906 Roosevelt visited the canal site to inspect the construction progress. He made the journey on the USS Louisiana from Piney Point, Maryland. The canal was officially opened in 1914.

Q: Who was the first president to fly regularly in the official jet aircraft known as Air Force One?

A: *John F. Kennedy.* Propeller planes were used to transport presidents beginning with the FDR administration, and the designation Air Force One was first used in 1953, but it was not until 1962 that Kennedy became the first president to fly regularly in his own jet aircraft, a modified Boeing 707. (Eisenhower took a goodwill tour at the end of his second term in a jet but it was not his usual mode of conveyance.) No matter where in the world the president travels, if he flies in an Air Force jet, the plane is called Air Force One. In practice, however, Air Force One is now used to refer to one of two highly customized Boeing 747-200B series aircraft.

Q: Which president was known for creating the first Kitchen Cabinet?

A: *Andrew Jackson.* During his presidency, Jackson was said to have relied more on informal advisors who dropped in on him at the White House than on the members of his official Cabinet. Several of these advisors, whom critics dubbed a Kitchen Cabinet, were either newspaper editors or personal friends of Jackson from Tennessee. The term continues to be used to describe unofficial advisors to the president.

Q: Who was the first president to name an African American to his cabinet?

A: *Lyndon Johnson.* Johnson appointed Robert Clifton Weaver of New York as secretary of Housing and Urban Development in 1966. He was the first African American cabinet member in the U.S. government. Weaver had served on FDR's so-called Black Cabinet, a group of African American policy advisors, earlier in his career. During his tenure as secretary, Weaver established the Model Cities program to help local authorities with urban renewal.

Q: Which president practiced "ping-pong" diplomacy?

A: *Richard Nixon.* Nixon took the bold step of putting aside America's long-time hostilities with China and making a gesture of peace. After diplomatic discussions with Chairman Mao Tse-tung began in 1971, Mao invited the U.S. ping-pong team to play China's national ping-pong team. Ping-pong diplomacy refers to the historic visit to China by the American sports delegation and the thawing of relations between the two world powers.

Souvenir ping-pong paddles with caricatures of Nixon and Mao, early 1970s.

Q: **Who was the first sitting president to visit Europe?**

A: *Woodrow Wilson.* Wilson crossed the Atlantic Ocean to attend a peace conference in Paris in 1919. The aim of the conference was to negotiate the terms of a treaty with Germany at the end of World War I. Wilson had already drawn up a plan called the Fourteen Points, which proposed "peace without victory." He hoped to create a League of Nations to maintain that peace. However, the Senate did not embrace Wilson's plan and failed to ratify the treaty.

Lalique brooch presented to the first lady during the Wilsons' historic visit to Paris, 1919.

Q: Which president was a champion of the conservation movement?

A: *Theodore Roosevelt.* After his first wife died in 1884, Roosevelt headed out to the Dakota Badlands and lived as a cowboy for several years. That experience gave him a love of nature. As twenty-sixth president, Roosevelt was a great conservationist. Under his leadership, some 230 million acres of land were placed under public protection through the addition of 150 national forests, 4 national game preserves, 18 national monuments, 51 federal bird reservations, and 5 national parks.

Q: Which president instituted the handshake as the official way to greet guests?

A: *Thomas Jefferson.* For presidents today, shaking hands is just part of the job. Each firm clasp could win a vote or charm a foreign dignitary. But Jefferson, who started the tradition, used it as a way to greet guests simply because it seemed more egalitarian than the formal bow employed by George Washington and John Adams. Jefferson had no consideration for status: ordinary citizens and high-ranking diplomats received the same unpretentious welcome to the White House.

Q: Which president forged a peace accord that ended three decades of war between Israel and Egypt?

A: *Jimmy Carter.* Carter hosted peace talks in 1978 between Prime Minister Menachem Begin of Israel and President Anwar Sadat of Egypt. After nearly two weeks of tense negotiations at Camp David, with a beaming Carter standing by, the two leaders signed a peace accord, which ended the state of war that had existed between their nations since 1948.

Q: Which first ladies were responsible for picking "Hail to the Chief" as the presidential theme song?

A: *Julia Tyler and Sarah Polk.* Tyler requested that the popular song "Hail to the Chief" be played whenever her husband entered a room, primarily to boost his image. Mrs. Polk later adopted it as well. It is said that James Polk was not an impressive figure and could walk into a room unnoticed. The song ensured that the president's entrance would not be missed. After these two administrations, the playing of "Hail to the Chief" for the president became a ritual.

Sheet music for the popular tune "Hail to the Chief," c. 1832.

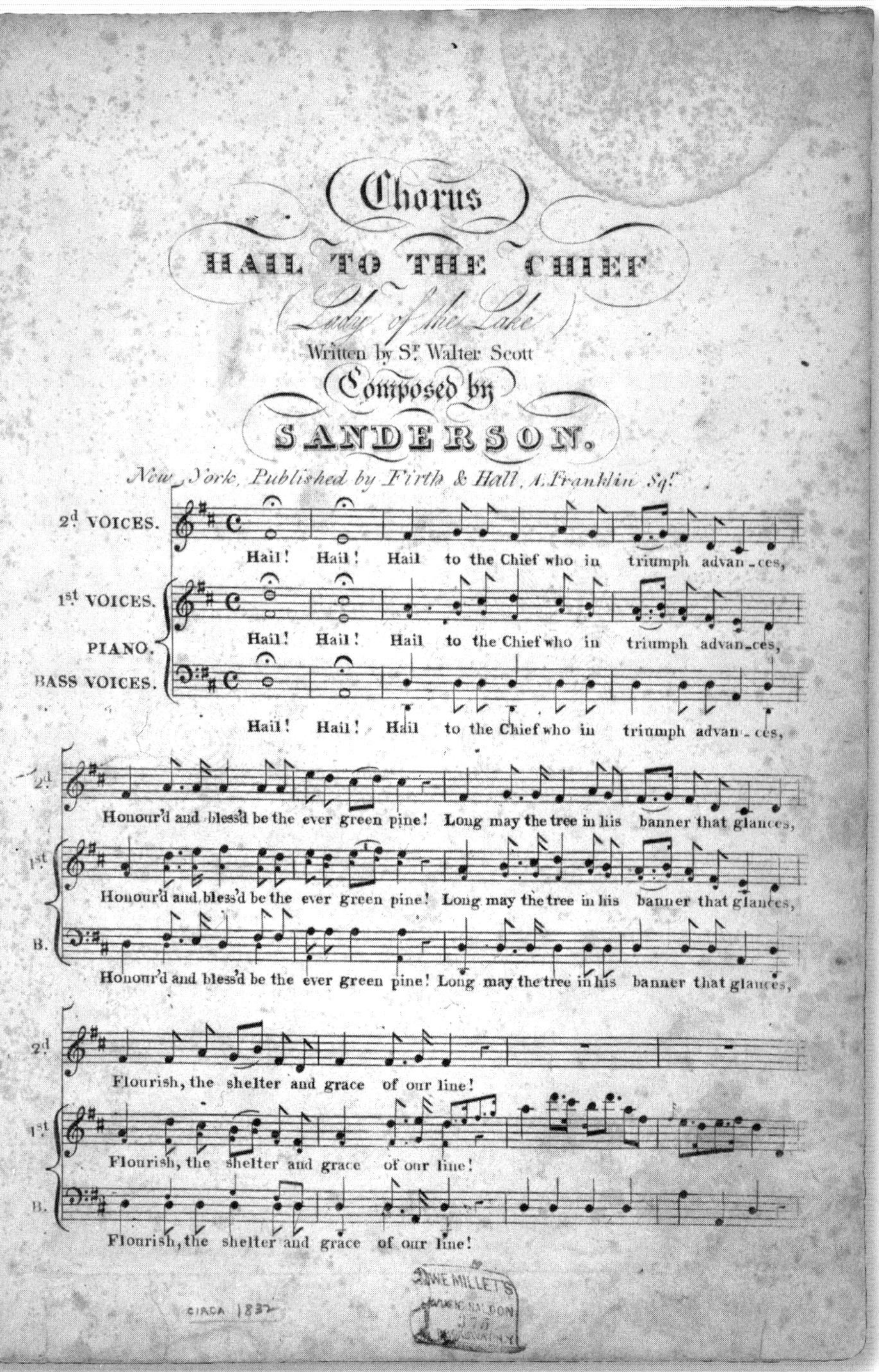
Chorus
HAIL TO THE CHIEF
(Lady of the Lake)
Written by Sr. Walter Scott
Composed by
SANDERSON.
New York, Published by Firth & Hall, 1 Franklin Sq.
2d VOICES.
Hail! Hail! Hail to the Chief who in triumph advan_ces,
1st VOICES.
PIANO.
Hail! Hail! Hail to the Chief who in triumph advan_ces,
BASS VOICES.
Hail! Hail! Hail to the Chief who in triumph advan_ces,
2d
Honour'd and bless'd be the ever green pine! Long may the tree in his banner that glances,
1st
Honour'd and bless'd be the ever green pine! Long may the tree in his banner that glances,
B.
Honour'd and bless'd be the ever green pine! Long may the tree in his banner that glances,
2d
Flourish, the shelter and grace of our line!
1st
Flourish, the shelter and grace of our line!
B.
Flourish, the shelter and grace of our line!
CIRCA 1837

Q: Who was the only president to authorize the use of atomic weapons?

A: *Harry Truman.* Truman authorized the dropping of two atomic bombs on Japan, primarily to avoid massive Allied casualties in that region and to hasten the end of World War II. On August 6, 1945, the bomber *Enola Gay* dropped the first bomb on the Japanese city of Hiroshima. More than 250,000 people are estimated to have been killed on impact or later by exposure to radioactivity. Later that day Truman wrote, "We have discovered the most terrible bomb in the history of the world."

Enola Gay, which dropped the first atomic bomb on Japan, August 6, 1945.

Q: Which president holds the record for most vetoes?

A: *Franklin D. Roosevelt.* Roosevelt wins the prize for the most vetoes with 635. However, he served three full terms, plus a few months into his fourth term as president. For two-term presidents, Grover Cleveland issued the most, at 584. Gerald Ford had the most vetoes for a one-term president with 66.

Q: Which presidents were responsible for forming the Democratic-Republican Party in the 1790s?

A: *Thomas Jefferson and James Madison.* George Washington called political parties "potent engines by which cunning, ambitious, and unprincipled men will be enabled to subvert the power of the people and to usurp for themselves the reins of government." Those who followed him, however, could not resist turning political factions into parties. Jefferson and Madison formed the Democratic-Republic Party to counter the Federalist Party of John Adams and Alexander Hamilton. Since then, several presidents have earned the office by building or reshaping political parties.

Q: **Who was president when the Nineteenth Amendment giving women the right to vote was signed into law?**

A: *Woodrow Wilson.* During World War I, women were of invaluable help to the war effort. The women's suffrage movement, which had long been lobbying to give women the vote, demanded that such work be rewarded with political equality. Wilson, who was not receptive to the suffragists before the war, declared in a speech on September 18, 1918, "We have made partners of the women in this war. Shall we admit them only to a partnership of suffering and sacrifice and toil and not to a partnership of right?" On August 26, 1920, the Nineteenth Amendment to the United States Constitution became law, enabling women to vote in that year's presidential election.

Jailed for Freedom pin, created to honor imprisoned women's suffrage activists, 1917.

Chapter 5

The Perpetual Podium

THE HARSH GLARE OF THE MEDIA

"[Journalists] are a sort of assassins who sit with leaded blunderbusses at the corners of streets and fire them off for hire or for sport at any passenger they select."

—*John Quincy Adams*

Some Account of some of the Bloody Deeds of

GEN. JACKSON.

Jacob Webb. David Morrow. John Harris. Henry Lewis. David Hunt. Edward Lindsey.

A brief account of the Execution of the Six Militia Men.

As we may soon expect to have the *official* documents in relation to the SIX MILITIA MEN, arrested, tried, and put to death, under the orders of General Andrew Jackson, this may not be an improper time to give to the public some of the particulars of their execution, as we have them from "AN EYE WITNESS," who appeals to Col. Russell, for the truth of every word he relates.

Harris was a Baptist preacher, with a large family. He had hired as a substitute for three months. This was the case with most of them. They were ignorant men, but obstinate in what they believed right, and what they had been told by their officers was right. They were all sure they could not be kept beyond three months, and they gave up their muskets, and had provisions dealt out to them, from the public stores, before they left the camp. This confirmed their convictions that they were right, and doing what was lawful.

Col. Russell commanded at the execution. The Militia men were brought to the place in a large wagon. The military dispositions being made, Col. Russell rode up to the wagon and ordered the men to descend. Harris was the only one who betrayed feminine weakness. The awfulness of the occasion; his wife and nine children; the parting with his son; and the fear of a quickly approaching ignominious death! quite overcome him, and he sunk in unmanly grief. No feeling of military pride could brace him up.

Col. Russell, doubtless, felt as a man, but he felt also for the pride of the army, and desired to animate the men with fortitude. "You are about to "die," said he, "by the sentence of a "Court Martial—die like men; *like soldiers*. You have been brave in the "field—you have fought well—do no "discredit to your country, or dishonor to the army, or yourselves, "by any unmanly fears. Meet your "fate with courage."

Harris attempted to make some apology for his conduct, but while he spoke, he wept bitterly. The fear of death, the idea that he should never again behold his wife and little ones, and his son weeping near him, had taken such entire possession of his mind that it was impossible he should rally.

Lewis, the gallant Lewis, said in a clear and manly tone, "Colonel, I "have served my country well. I "love it dearly, and would, if I could, "serve it longer and better. I have "fought bravely—you know I have, and "HERE I have a right to say so "MYSELF. I would not wish to die in "this way"—here his voice faltered, "and he passed the back of his right "hand over his eyes—" I did not expect it. But I am now as firm as I "have been in battle, and you shall see "that I will die as becomes a soldier; "you know I am a brave man." "Yes, Lewis," said the Colonel, "you "have always behaved like a brave "man." Other sentences were uttered, other declarations were made, and words of comfort spoken, but they were lost on me; my attention, says an Eye Witness, being chiefly directed to Lewis.

Six coffins were ranged as directed, and on each of them knelt one of our condemned American Militia Men. Such a sight was never seen before! I trust to God it never will be seen again! Six soldiers were detailed and drawn up to fire at each man. What an awful duty! Their white caps were drawn over the faces of the unhappy men. Harris evidently trembled, and I could almost persuade myself that the heart of Lewis was enlarged, and that his bosom rose with manly courage to meet death. The fatal word was given and they all fell.

As we approached the scene of blood and carnage, Lewis gave signs of life; the rest were all dead—he crawled upon his coffin. After the lapse of a few minutes, he said—I give his very words: "Colonel!"—the Colonel was close to him—"Colonel, I "am not killed, but I am sadly cut "and mangled." His body was now examined, and it was found that but four balls had wounded him. "Col- "onel, said he, "did I behave well?" "Yes, Lewis," said the Colonel in the kindest tone of voice, "like a man."—"Well, sir," said he, "have I not "atoned for this offence? *Shall I not "live?*" The Colonel was much agitated, and gave orders that the Surgeon should, if possible, preserve his life. They did all that skill and humanity could do—it was all of no avail. Poor Lewis expressed a great desire to live—"not," said he at one time, "that I fear death, but I would repent "me of some sins, and I desire to live "yet a little longer in the world." He suffered inconceivable agony from his wounds and died on the fourth day.

Many a soldier has wept over his grave. He was a brave man and much beloved. He suffered twenty deaths. I have seen the big drops chase each other down his forehead with pain and anguish. There was much sensibility and sympathy throughout the camp. I would not have, unjustly and unnecessarily, signed this death warrant for all the wealth of all the Indies. The soldiers detailed to shoot Lewis had, from strong feelings of sympathy, or mistaken humanity, failed to shoot him—but four balls had entered his body.

"An Eye Witness" appeals to Col. Russell, who he thinks now lives in Alabama, for the perfect truth of this sketch. He does not fear but the Colonel will keenly recollect and faithfully depict the horrors of the day on which six Americans were shot to death under his command—but not by his orders.

The order bears date the very day after *General Jackson* returned in triumph to New Orleans, and the day before he joyfully went, under triumphal arches, to the temple of the living God; where, says the historian, "they *crowned* their adored General with laurels." The order for the execution of these six unhappy men bears date January 22, 1815. His crown of laurels had not yet withered when blood, the life's blood of his countrymen, of his fellow soldiers, flowed plentifully by his order. May that order and its consequences, sink deep into the hearts of the American people, and steel them against him who had no flesh in his obdurate heart; who did not feel for Man; in the midst of Joy and Revelry, almost in the more immediate presence of his Creator, who issued the fatal order to put his fellow creatures to death, and to make their wives and children, widows and orphans.

MOURNFUL TRAGEDY;

Or, the death of Jacob Webb, David Morrow, John Harris, Henry Lewis, David Hunt and Edward Lindsey—six militia men—who were condemned to die, the sentence approved by Major General JACKSON, and by his order the whole six shot.

O! did you hear that plaintive cry
Borne on the southern breeze?
Saw you John Harris earnest pray
For mercy, on his knees?

Low to the earth he bent, and pray'd
For pardon from his chief;
But to his earnest prayer for life
JACKSON, alas! was deaf.

"Spare me," he said, "I mean no wrong,
"My heart was always true;
"First for my country's cause it beat,
"And next, great Chief, for you.

"We thought our time of service out—
"Thought it our right to go;
"We meant to violate no law,
"Nor wish'd to shun the foe.

"Our officers declar'd that we
"Had but three months to stay;
"We serv'd those three months faithfully
"Up to the latest day.

"No one suspects intended wrong;
"The judgment only err'd;
"In such a case, O noble Chief,
"Let mercy's voice be heard.

"At home an aged mother waits
"To clasp her only son;
"A wife, and little children—this arm
"Alone depend upon.

"Cut me not off from those dear ties!
"So soon from life's young bloom:
"O 'tis a dreadful thing to die,
"And moulder in the tomb!

"Sure mercy is a noble gem
"In every Chieftain's brow;
"More sparkling than a diadem—
"O exercise it now!"—

'Twas all in vain, John Harris' pray'r,
'Tis past the soul's belief!
Hard as the flint was Jackson's heart;
He would not grant relief.

He order'd Harris out to die,
And five poor fellows more!
Young, gallant men, in prime of life,
To welter in their gore!!

Methinks I hear the muffled drum,
And see the column move;
Lo here they come—how sad their looks!
Farewell to life and love!

See six black coffins rang'd along—
Six graves before them made;
Webb, Lindsey, Harris, Lewis, Hunt,
And Morris kneel'd and pray'd.

They kneel'd, & pray'd, & tho't of home,
And all its dear delights—
The deadly tubes are level'd now—
The scene my soul affrights!

Sure he will spare! Sure JACKSON yet
Will all reprieve but one—
O hark! those shrieks! that cry of death!
The dreadful deed is done!

All six militia men were shot;
And O! it seems to me
A dreadful deed—a bloody act
Of needless cruelty.

The reader is reminded that it was on the 21st day of January, 1815, that General Jackson returned to the city of New Orleans from the battle ground. The British had abandoned the enterprise and retired. The General was received with the strongest demonstrations of joy and attachment. It was on that very day, January 21, that he issued the order for the execution of the six militia-men. The 23d was appointed a day of general thanksgiving, when the General was provided with a wreath of Laurel by the hands of the Bishop. On the 28th of the same month an order was issued for the execution of twelve soldiers, condemned by a Court Martial at Nashville. All to be executed within four days after the promulgation of the order!!

"(Extract from the General Order, dated 'Adjutant General's Office, New Orleans, January 28th, 1815, Head Quarters, 7th Military District,' on the proceedings of the General Court Martial, held at Nashville on the 19th of October, 1814, and continued by adjournment till the 25th of November, 1814.)"

"Was also tried the following-named men, soldiers of the army of the United States, severally charged with 'desertion,' viz.: Richard Wall, of 3d Rifle Regiment; Jacob Perregrin, of said Regiment: both of Capt. Willey Martin's company; John Jones, of the 24th Regiment of Infantry; William Myers, of Capt. Humphrey's company of Artillery; Jacob King, of Capt. Reed's company, said corps; Benjamin Harris, of the 44th Infantry; John Young, of the 39th Infantry; Nathaniel Chester, of the corps of Artillery; Drury Puckett, of the 24th Infantry; Wyat Grantt, of the 39th Infantry; Joseph Muckelroy, of the 24th Infantry; and James McBride, 2d Rifle Regiment; to which charge they severally pleaded Not Guilty, except Jacob King, who pleaded Guilty. The Court, after the examination of testimony on each of the cases, and deliberation had thereon, pronounce on each and every one of them 'Death by shooting.' The Major General approves the sentence passed on the above named soldiers of the Army of the United States, and orders the same to be carried into full effect in four days after the promulgation of this order, at the post where they may be, under the direction of the senior officer present."

Another was to have been executed at the same time. He was a young man, who had deserted one month before his time had expired. General Jackson doomed him to die with the others. He was saved by a writ of habeas corpus from Judge M'Nairy, who fell under Jackson's displeasure for snatching this one victim from his blood stained hands. If Jackson's army had been at hand, no doubt M'Nairy would have shared the fate of Judge Hall and Judge Fromentin. Capital punishments in an army, are designed for example as well as for penalty; but in this case it was a transaction of horror to peaceful citizens: no army was there to witness the bloody tragedy. He has ever been a man of "blood and carnage."

There can be no doubt that every one of those men were executed. There was no power to save them after the promulgation of this order. Thus we see that Gen. Jackson, within the space of one week, in the midst of exultations and rejoicings, ordered eighteen of his fellow men to be put to death!!! Is there any instance on record, in any history of modern warfare, that equals this for barbarity? The time, the circumstances, the numbers. And can it be that this barbarian shall be elevated to the chief magistracy of a free, a generous, and a merciful nation?

Do not be startled, gentle reader, at the picture before you. It is all true and every body ought to know it. Gen. Jackson having made an assault upon Samuel Jackson, in the streets of Nashville, and the latter not being disposed to stand still and be beaten, stooped down for a stone to defend himself—While in the act of doing so, Gen. Jackson drew the sword from his cane and run it thro' Sam'l Jackson's body, the sword entering his back and coming out of his breast. For this offence an indictment was found against Gen. Jackson, by a grand jury, upon which he was subsequently arraigned and tried. But finding means to persuade the petit jury that he committed the act in self defence, he was acquitted. Gentle reader, it is for you to say, whether this man, who carries a sword cane, and is willing to run it thro' the body of any one who may presume to stand in his way, is a fit person to be our President.

Poor JOHN WOODS; he was a generous hearted, noble fellow as ever lived, who had volunteered in the service of his country. He was on guard one day at Fort Strother—the officer of the guard had permitted him to go to his tent, and snatch a hasty breakfast; whilst disposing of his scanty meal, seated on the ground beside his skillet, an upstart little officer, who was not Wood's equal at home, ordered him to pick up and carry off some bones that lay scattered about the place—Woods refused, and the little officer attempted to compel him. At this instant, Gen. Jackson, having heard the dispute, came out of his tent, and without knowing any thing of the merits of the case, repeatedly vociferated—"*Shoot the damn'd rascal!—Shoot the damn'd rascal.*" For this offence, the unfortunate, the gallant Woods, was tried, condemned and shot. Before his trial, Gen. Jackson used this language to the court-martial. "*By the immortal God! if you find him guilty I will not pardon him!*" And he kept his promise; though he did offer a pardon provided he would enlist in the regular service—Thus perished as noble a fellow as ever lived, for as trifling an offence as ever took the life of man!!!

On the 27th day of March, 1814, General Jackson had found at an Indian village, at the bend of the Tallapoosa, about 4000 Indians, with their *squaws and children*, "running about among their huts." The following is an account of the sanguinary massacre which took place—it is Gen. Jackson's own, and therefore must be received as sufficient evidence against himself. He says:—"DETERMINING TO EXTERMINATE them, I detached Gen. Coffee with the mounted men and nearly the whole of the Indian force, early on the morning of yesterday, to cross the river about two miles below the encampment, that none of them should escape by attempting to cross the river." The result he then details:—"*Five hundred and fifty-seven were left dead on the Peninsula, and a great number of them were killed by the horsemen attempting to cross the river.* IT IS BELIEVED THAT NO MORE THAN TEN ESCAPED. WE CONTINUED TO DESTROY *many of them who had concealed themselves under the banks of the river, until we were prevented by the night.* THIS MORNING WE KILLED 16 WHICH HAD BEEN CONCEALED."

We ask you to pause and reflect that the above tragic narration of cold blooded and merciless cruelty, is taken from an official communication, made by General Andrew Jackson.

The General, after sleeping (with what composure, we cannot say) through the night ensuing the tragedy we speak of, awoke in the morning surrounded by the corpses of "five hundred and seventy" fellow creatures, to cause, by way of worthy afterpiece, sixteen others to be dragged from their concealments, and put to death in cold blood. We cannot boast of more than common sensibility, but we must think that to witness such an act, would make ours a little cold also. What are the general's words?—these: "this morning we killed sixteen which had been concealed!"—and the man who acts and speaks thus, who has half as much blood upon his conscience, as he has upon his hands—he, forsooth, is to be called the peer and *like* of Washington, the happy warrior,——————" he Whom every man at arms could wish to be."

But it is time to have done with the unpleasant subject. We will observe in addition to the details already given, that the village was burnt, and several women and children killed. In conclusion, we ask our fellow citizens, whether Gen. Jackson though he has contributed largely to the military reputation of our country, has not done enough to disqualify him, in the eyes of the *people* as virtuous as they are free, for the office he seeks at their hands.

Gen. Jackson, detailing his progress among the Indians, in the course of which, men, WOMEN and CHILDREN, were indiscriminately "exterminated," their towns burnt, and their country laid waste, with the utmost complacency and *sang froid*, says, in his letter dated, "Camp before St. Marks, April 9, 1818—"Captain McKever having hoisted English colours on board of his boats, Francis *the Prophet*, Hoemochemutcho, and *two others*, were *decoyed* on board. *These have been hung to-day!*" Reader, mark the perfect indifference with which Gen. Jackson shoots, hangs or stabs his fellow beings, with or without trial, and the more than callous, aye, even exulting composure, with which he details his horrid and bloody deeds! If the Indians, according to the customs of their nation, put to death a prisoner, all the feelings of our nature rise into indignation against them. With what feelings then should we contemplate the *decoying* & the cold-blooded murder of prisoners, by a civilized man, in the face of the laws and customs of his country.

FRANKLIN, Tenn. September 10, 1813.

A difference which had been for some months brewing between Gen. Jackson and myself, produced on Saturday, 4th inst. in the town of Nashville, the most outrageous affray ever witnessed in a civilized country. In communicating the affair to my friends and fellow citizens, I limit myself to the statement of a few leading facts, the truth of which I am ready to establish by judicial proofs.

1. That myself and my brother, Jesse Benton, arriving in Nashville on the morning of the affray, and knowing of Gen. Jackson's threats, went and took lodgings in a different house from the one in which he staid, on purpose to avoid him.

2. That the Gen. and some of his friends came to the house where we had put up and commenced the attack by leveling a pistol at me, when I had no weapon drawn, and advancing upon me at a quick pace without giving me time to draw one.

3. That seeing this, my brother fired upon Gen. Jackson, when he had got within eight or ten feet of me.

4. That four other pistols were fired in quick succession; one by Gen. Jackson at me; two by me at the Gen.; and one by Col. Coffee at me. In the course of this firing, Gen. Jackson was brought to the ground; but received no hurt.

5. That daggers were then drawn. Col. Coffee and Mr. Alexander Donaldson made at me, and gave me five slight wounds. Capt. Hammond and Mr. Stokeley Hays engaged my brother, who, being still weak from the effects of a severe wound he had lately received in a duel, was not able to resist two men. They got him down; and while Capt. Hammond beat him on the head to make him lie still, Mr. Hays attempted to stab him, and wounded him in both arms, as he lay on his back parrying the thrusts with his naked hands. From this situation a generous hearted citizen of Nashville, Mr. Summer, relieved him. Before he came to the ground, my brother clapped a pistol to the breast of Mr. Hays to blow him through, but it missed fire.

6. My own and my brother's pistols carried two balls each; for it was our intention, if driven to arms, to have no child's play. The pistols fired at me were so near that the blaze of the muzzle of one of them burnt the sleeve of my coat, and the other, aimed at my head at a little more than arm's length from it.

7. Capt. Carroll was to have taken part in the affray, but was absent by the permission of Gen. Jackson, as he has proved by the General's certificate; a certificate which reflects I know not whether less honour upon the General or upon the Captain.

8. That this attack was made upon me in the house where the Judge of the District, Mr. Searcy, had his lodgings! Nor has the civil authority yet taken cognisance of this horrible outrage.

These facts are sufficient to fix the public opinion. For my own part, I think it scandalous that such things should take place at any time; but particularly so at the present moment, when the public service requires the aid of all its citizens. As for the name of *courage*, God forbid that I should ever attempt to gain it by becoming a bully. Those who know me, know full well that I would give a thousand times more for the reputation of *Croghan* in defending his post, than I would for the reputation of all the duelists and gladiators that ever appeared upon the face of the earth.

THOMAS HART BENTON, *Lieut. Col. Thirty-Ninth Infantry*

And now a member of the Senate of the United States.

Q: Which president was accused of having blood on his hands by the political press?

A: *Andrew Jackson.* Jackson was the subject of a particularly vicious political broadside (a nineteenth-century version of a negative campaign ad) accusing him of the execution of six militiamen during the War of 1812. Widely distributed by Jackson's opponents, it caused a scandal during the campaign of 1828 and put Jackson supporters on the defensive.

Broadside, 1828, showing six coffins for the militiamen supposedly executed by Jackson during the War of 1812.

Q: **Who was the first president to use a Teleprompter?**

A: *Dwight Eisenhower.* Eisenhower, however, wasn't totally comfortable using one. Subsequent commanders in chief have used Teleprompters for important speeches and addresses with varying success. Barack Obama has made the greatest use of them, even employing Teleprompters for everyday announcements and opening statements at news conferences.

Q: **Who was the first president to establish regularly scheduled press conferences?**

A: *Woodrow Wilson.* Wilson instituted regular and formal press conferences. He saw them as a way to influence public opinion, but he also thought that communication via the press was part of what constituted a democratic society. Since his time, all presidents have held formal press conferences, but each administration has decided how many to hold and how frequent they should be. Presidents can control the media by choosing a time, place, and even the participants at a press conference.

Q: Which president was called His Fraudulency?

A: *Rutherford B. Hayes.* The press called Republican president Hayes His Fraudulency because he "stole" the 1876 election from Democrat Samuel Tilden. Hayes won the election by one electoral vote, after much controversy in which thousands of ballots were disputed and some ruled invalid. With the results in several states completely unclear and with competing slates of electors attempting to cast votes for their own candidates, Congress chose to appoint an Electoral Commission to decide the election. After Tilden was declared the loser, Southern Democrats were so outraged that they declared they would not accept Hayes's leadership unless he removed the federal troops that had occupied the South since the Civil War.

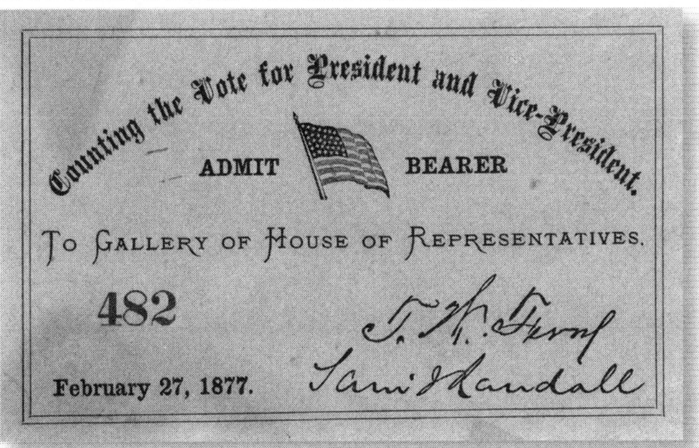

Counting the Vote for President and Vice-President.
ADMIT
BEARER
To Gallery of House of Representatives.
482
February 27, 1877.
T. W. Ferry
Sam'l Randall

Ticket to view the re-count of electoral votes in the disputed Hayes-Tilden election, 1877.

Q: **Who was the only president who refused to attend the annual dinner of the Gridiron Club?**

A: *Grover Cleveland.* Cleveland was openly hostile to the press and did not give newsmen working space in the White House. When a journalist asked the president to appoint a new secretary who might be good to newspapermen, Cleveland responded: "I have a notion to appoint a man who will be good to me." Cleveland remains the only president who refused to attend the annual dinner of the Gridiron Club, the insider association of Washington journalists founded in 1885, which has a good-natured "roast" of the president each year. Barack Obama was unable to appear in 2009 and 2010 due to scheduling conflicts, but attended in 2011.

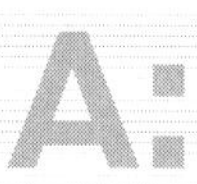

Which president was called the Great Communicator?

A: *Ronald Reagan.* One could say that Reagan had been auditioning for the role of president most of his life. He was a Hollywood actor in his youth and then became president of the Screen Actors Guild before going into politics. Reagan loved the camera and was master of the quick quip and memorable sound bite. His effective use of television to promote his programs earned him the nickname the Great Communicator.

Q: Which president's campaign gave birth to a major newspaper?

A: *William Henry Harrison's. The Log Cabin* was a newspaper created by Horace Greeley to promote Harrison's candidacy. Greeley continued to publish after Harrison's election and eventually turned the publication into the *New-York Tribune*. The *Tribune* was known for its reformist platform and ran scathing anti-slavery editorials before and during the Civil War. Greeley published the *Tribune* until his death in 1872.

The Log Cabin campaign newspaper, which later became the *New-York Tribune*, 1840.

THE LOG CABIN.

PUBLISHED SIMULTANEOUSLY IN NEW-YORK AND ALBANY.

BY H. GREELEY & CO. SATURDAY, JULY 25, 1840. VOLUME I. NO. 15.

Q: Who was the first president to deliver a speech by radio?

A: *Warren Harding.* On June 14, 1922, Harding became the first president to have his voice transmitted by radio. The president was addressing a crowd in Baltimore at the dedication of a memorial to Francis Scott Key, the composer of "The Star-Spangled Banner." Harding was also the first president to have a radio installed at the White House.

Harding getting his point across, photo by Herbert E. French, c. 1920.

Q: Which president was called the Human Iceberg?

A: *Benjamin Harrison.* For a president, Harrison was seriously lacking in social skills. He hated small talk and was stiff and awkward in public. With no charisma and warmth to his name, he was mocked as the Human Iceberg. On the positive side, Harrison was known to be intelligent, honest, and of the highest integrity. He was also a proficient speaker.

Q: Who was the first president seen on television?

A: *Franklin D. Roosevelt.* In April 1939, at the opening of the World's Fair in New York City, Roosevelt made history by becoming the first president to be seen on TV. The broadcast was produced by the National Broadcasting Company (NBC), which used mobile camera trucks to transmit the program to a receiver atop an aerial on the Empire State Building. The ceremony was watched by a few hundred viewers on receivers inside the RCA pavilion at the Fair as well as in the Radio City building in Manhattan. It would be another decade before TV became a fixture in American households.

Q: Which president was called the Little Magician?

A: *Martin Van Buren.* Van Buren was five feet six inches—and a crafty politician. The eighth president was known for keeping his opinions to himself, which left both supporters and opponents in doubt as to his true motives. Such slyness earned him the title Little Magician. His other nickname was The Red Fox of Kinderhook. (He hailed from Kinderhook, New York.)

Q: Which president made a joke that almost started a war with Russia?

A: *Ronald Reagan.* On August 11, 1984, Reagan joked during a sound check for his Saturday radio address, "My fellow Americans, I'm pleased to tell you today that I've signed legislation that will outlaw Russia forever. We begin bombing in five minutes." Those in the room laughed at the president's quip, but a tape soon leaked. The Soviets briefly put forces on high alert. Embarrassed U.S. officials quickly assured the Kremlin that Reagan's offhand remark did not reflect White House policy.

Q: Who was the first president to make a telecast from the Capitol?

A: *Harry Truman.* Truman's State of the Union address on January 6, 1947, is notable for being the first one to be televised. In his characteristic lighthearted way, Truman, a Democrat, began, "It looks like a good many of you have moved over to the left since I was here last!" Truman was referring to the fact that Republicans had recently gained 55 seats in Congress. Although they sat in their customary position on the right side of the House chamber, from Truman's vantage point at the podium, they were on the left.

Badge celebrating Truman's inauguration, January 1949.

Q: Which president's dog was the first White House pet to become a media star?

A: *Warren Harding's Airedale terrier Laddie Boy.* Laddie Boy was the first first dog to receive regular coverage from the media. He was six months old when he arrived at the White House. In 1921, the newspapers gave him almost daily coverage, with headlines like "Gets Airedale as Mascot," "Laddie Boy a Newsboy," "Trees White House Cat," "Laddie Boy Gets Playmate." Harding took such pleasure in Laddie Boy that he had one thousand bronze miniatures made in the dog's image shortly after taking office.

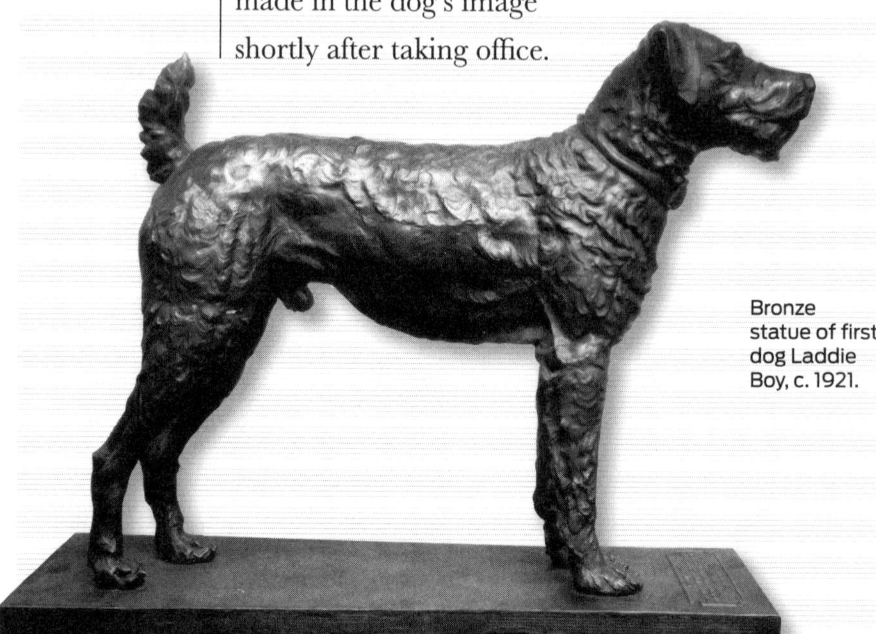

Bronze statue of first dog Laddie Boy, c. 1921.

Q: Who was the first president to appear in a political ad on TV?

A: *Dwight Eisenhower.* During the 1952 campaign, Eisenhower was persuaded that short ads played during popular TV programs such as *I Love Lucy* would do more to win over voters than any other form of advertising. His opponent, Adlai Stevenson, didn't agree, saying, "The idea that you can merchandise candidates for high office like breakfast cereal is the ultimate indignity to the democratic process." Stevenson lost two races against Ike—in 1952 and 1956.

Q: Which first lady won an Emmy Award?

A: *Jackie Kennedy.* An honorary Emmy was awarded to Kennedy for her televised tour of the White House in 1962. Normally publicity shy, the first lady was encouraged to make the broadcast to show the public the restoration work she had undertaken at the Executive Mansion. Reviews of her hour-long TV tour were glowing, and the National Academy of Television Arts and Sciences subsequently honored her achievement.

Q: Which first lady was called Steel Magnolia?

A: *Rosalynn Carter.* Was she a delicate flower or tough as nails? Some reporters saw Carter's Southern charm as a thin veil for her strong will and determination. As first lady, she was very active in the day-to-day affairs of her husband's administration—even sometimes attending cabinet meetings and serving on the President's Commission on Mental Health. She also represented the Carter administration on an official trip to Latin America. That led to questions about the role of a first lady and whether she had exceeded the limits of her position.

Q: Which president held the first televised news conference?

A: *John F. Kennedy.* On January 25, 1961, JFK became the first president to hold a live televised news conference. The charismatic president read a prepared statement regarding the famine in the Congo, the release of two American aviators from Russian custody, and impending negotiations for an atomic test ban treaty. Afterward, he opened the floor for questions from reporters. He addressed queries on a variety of topics, including relations with Cuba, voting rights, and aid to impoverished Americans.

Q: Who was the first chief executive to appear on newsreel while president?

A: *William McKinley.* The newsreel of McKinley's 1901 inaugural is grainy and lacks the subtle editing that characterizes modern film, but it's a wonderful record of the swearing-in of the twenty-fifth president. Six months later McKinley was assassinated and Theodore Roosevelt became president.

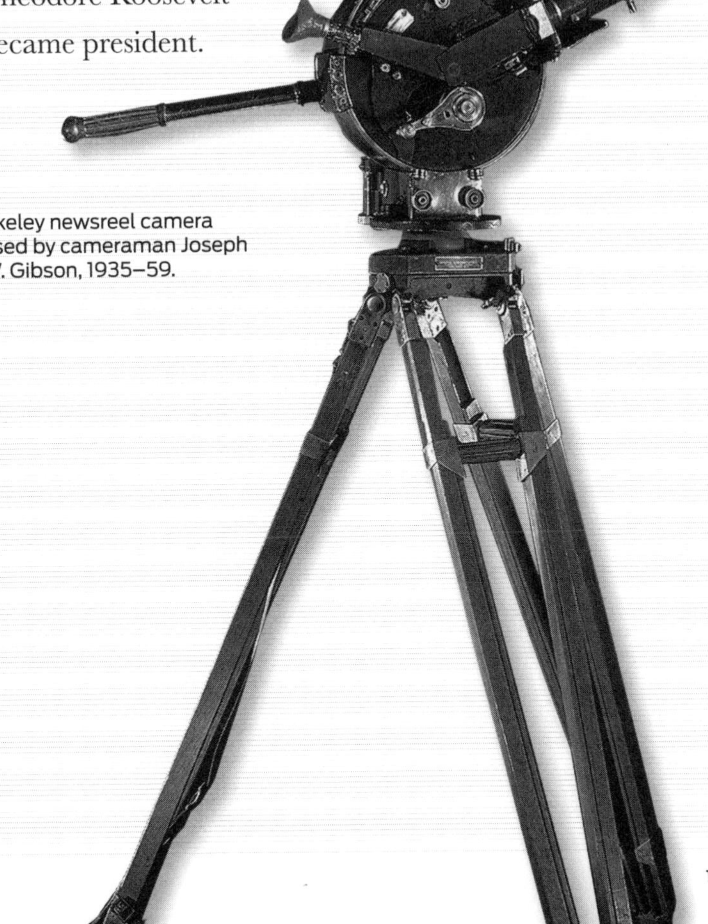

Akeley newsreel camera used by cameraman Joseph W. Gibson, 1935–59.

Q: **Which president earned the nickname Tricky Dick?**

A: *Richard Nixon.* Long before he resigned in the wake of the Watergate scandal, Nixon had his ups and downs in politics. He was elected to Congress in 1946 and ascended to the Senate in 1950. He served as Eisenhower's vice president, lost a bid for the presidency in 1960, and was elected to it in 1968. His campaign techniques and political maneuverings were seen by some as devious and dishonest, earning him the sobriquet Tricky Dick.

Q: **Who established the first White House pressroom?**

A: *Theodore Roosevelt.* In the early 1900s Roosevelt made the White House press corps a true institution when he gave reporters a designated office in a new executive office building, later known as the West Wing, and issued press credentials to certain members. This act gave the press unprecedented access to the president.

Q: Which first lady was the first to have a federally funded social secretary?

A: *Edith Roosevelt.* Not only was Edith married to Theodore Roosevelt, one of the most energetic men to hold the office of president, but she also had six rambunctious children at the White House. The demands of her marriage, her job as first lady, and her role as mother made it necessary for Edith to employ a social secretary to keep her schedule and coordinate calendars and responsibilities among other members of government and their wives.

Edith Roosevelt with her youngest child, Quentin, 1902.

Q: Whose State of the Union address was the first to be broadcast on radio?

A: *Calvin Coolidge's.* Coolidge made his first public radio broadcast—a speech to Congress later known as the State of the Union address—on December 6, 1923. The broadcast was a great success, and the president's voice was heard loud and clear—maybe too loud for some. A radio station in St. Louis—KSD—phoned the Capitol to ask what the grating noise was in the background. The tech guys at the Capitol answered, "That's the rustling of the paper as he turns the pages of his message."

Q: Which first lady won a Grammy Award for her best-selling audio book?

A: *Hillary Clinton.* Clinton won a Grammy for the recorded version of *It Takes a Village, and Other Lessons Children Teach Us*, her 1996 bestselling book. The book presents her vision of a society that works together to meet children's needs.

Q: Who installed the first telegraph office in the White House?

A: *Andrew Johnson.* The office areas of the White House were remodeled in 1866. At that time, Johnson had the first telegraph installed in a room next to his office. Later in his term, an electric bell system was also installed in the White House, which connected the upper floors to the servants' hall.

Q: Who was the first first lady to substitute for the president in his weekly radio address?

A: *Laura Bush.* Although she was not always known as an outspoken first lady, Bush became, in November 2001, the first first lady to give the president's weekly radio address. In her speech, she assailed the Taliban's oppression of women and children in Afghanistan.

Q: Who was the first president to make use of the Internet?

A: *Bill Clinton.* Aside from being Internet savvy on a personal level, on June 24, 2000, Clinton made the first webcast by a U.S. president. His remarks included the announcement of a new website that would enable citizens to search all government resources in one place and make government information easily available to the public.

Q: Which president used radio to chat directly with the public rather than communicate through the press corps?

A: *Franklin D. Roosevelt.* The author of the New Deal was the first president to regularly and effectively communicate by radio. By the early 1930s the National Broadcasting Company (NBC) and the Columbia Broadcasting System (CBS) were fixtures in American homes. FDR's "fireside chats" used the airwaves to talk directly to citizens in their own living rooms. Listeners felt close to Roosevelt, who used his broadcasts to calm their fears about the banking crisis during the Depression and allay their anxiety throughout World War II.

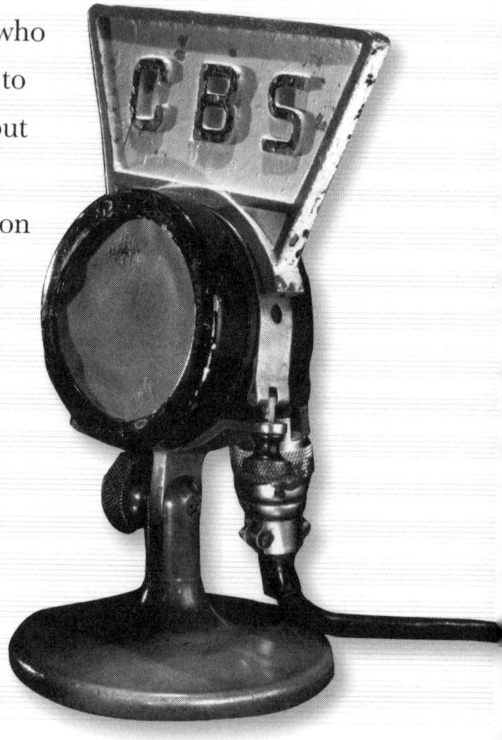

CBS radio microphone used by FDR during a "fireside chat," c. 1930s.

Q: Which president made the first telecast in color?

A: *Dwight Eisenhower.* On June 7, 1955, the president gave a televised address to the West Point class of 1955 on the fortieth anniversary of his graduation from West Point. The only U.S. presidents to graduate from West Point were Ulysses S. Grant and Eisenhower. Both were generals and both were Republicans.

Q: Who was the first first lady to speak openly about her treatment for cancer?

A: *Betty Ford.* Ford unexpectedly became first lady when Richard Nixon resigned in August 1974 and Gerald Ford was sworn in as his successor. She approached her new role eagerly and openly, holding her first formal press conference on September 4, 1974. She straightforwardly answered questions about women in politics, abortion rights, and a proposed Equal Rights Amendment to the Constitution—all of which endeared her to the public but caused controversy as well. A few weeks later, after being diagnosed with breast cancer, she again made history by discussing details of her diagnosis and treatment in public. Her candor helped raise public awareness about the disease and reassured many women battling cancer.

Q: Which first lady reclaimed her reputation with the media at the Gridiron Club?

A: *Nancy Reagan.* Reagan was often criticized for her expensive tastes but she met that criticism head-on in 1982. For that year's Gridiron Club dinner—an annual Washington affair where the press and politicians lampoon one another—she appeared in a navy polka-dotted blouse topped with a red print housedress and a blue Hawaiian print skirt, while wearing a pair of yellow galoshes. She belted out the tune "Second Hand Clothes" to the tune of "Second Hand Rose." It was a sensation and helped mend some fences between her and the media.

Nancy Reagan, in costume, taking the stage at the Gridiron Club, 1982.

Q: Which first lady hosted the first White House webcast?

A: *Hillary Clinton.* Clinton initiated the Millennium Project, a series of monthly lectures that considered America's past and forecast its future. The talks were held in the East Room of the White House. One of these became the first live webcast from the mansion.

Q: Which president had a special console of three televisions installed in the Oval Office?

A: *Lyndon Johnson.* Johnson used television as a major source of information and had a bank of three TVs installed in the Oval Office so that he could monitor the nightly newscasts of NBC, ABC, and CBS. Johnson also had TVs at his ranch in Texas, but poor reception was a problem, requiring that a tower be built to improve the quality.

Q: Who was the first sitting president to disclose his serious health condition to the media?

A: *Dwight Eisenhower.* In September 1955, Eisenhower suffered a heart attack and was immediately hospitalized. After he stabilized, Eisenhower instructed his press secretary to share details of his illness with the press, a complete departure from other administrations, which had worked to shield the country from bad news about the president's health. Eisenhower bore his illness like a general, and even wore red pajamas with five stars on the collar. His recovery was not as complete as it seemed, however. Although he was back on the job in less than two months, his health was still on shaky ground—a matter not disclosed to the public.

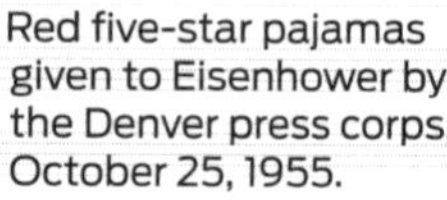

Red five-star pajamas given to Eisenhower by the Denver press corps, October 25, 1955.

Chapter 6

Home, Hotel, Parlor, and Playground

LIFE IN THE WHITE HOUSE

"It seems like there was always someone for dinner."

—*Harry Truman*, *on life in the White House*

Q: Which president had a putting green set up on the White House lawn and a driving range installed in the basement?

A: *Dwight Eisenhower.*

The general was an avid golfer, so much so that some members of Congress complained that he spent too much time on his swing and not enough time in the Oval Office. He managed to play once or twice a week while in office, and had a putting green and driving range installed so he could practice whenever possible.

Eisenhower's five-star golf bag with a partial set of clubs, 1960s.

Q: **Who was the first president to have a bowling alley at the White House?**

A: *Harry Truman.* The bowling alley, which was ready for use on April 25, 1947, was a gift from Truman's fellow Missourians. White House employees soon started a bowling league, which did not include the president, who preferred playing poker. Dwight Eisenhower closed the lanes in 1955, but in 1969 Richard Nixon had a new one-lane alley installed beneath the North Portico entrance, where it still exists today.

Q: **Which president had fifteen children?**

A: *John Tyler.* Tyler was married twice. He had eight children with his first wife, Letitia. After she died, the fifty-four-year-old president married the twenty-four-year-old Julia Gardiner, with whom he had seven more children. Tyler wins the prize for being the most prolific of all American presidents.

Q: Who was the only president to be married at the White House?

A: *Grover Cleveland.* Cleveland, at the age of forty-nine, married twenty-one-year-old Frances Folsom at the White House on June 2, 1886. The wedding made national headlines and the public was hungry for details. *The Washington Post* reported: "The bride wore an enchanting white dress of ivory satin, simply garnished on the high corsage with India muslin crossed in Grecian folds and carried in exquisite falls of simplicity over the petticoat." The dress is now in the Smithsonian's National Museum of American History.

Satin and lace cake box and card signed by the bride and groom, from the Cleveland-Folsom wedding, June 2, 1886.

Q: Which president was the first to hire a valet?

A: *Chester Arthur.* The president known as Elegant Arthur was a fashionable dresser and hired a personal valet to help him with his attire, becoming the first president to do so. He was said to own eighty pairs of pants and changed his clothes several times a day. Arthur's wife died before he took office and, with no first lady to oversee official events, he often made arrangements on his own. With the help of Louis Tiffany, a noted designer of the day and the son of Tiffany & Co. founder Charles Lewis Tiffany, he also refurbished the White House to suit his tastes.

Q: Which president attended séances in the White House?

A: *Abraham Lincoln.* Lincoln's wife, Mary Lincoln, became interested in séances after their young son Willie died in 1862. At the White House, she engaged mediums, who conducted "spirit circles" or ceremonies during which those who attended could communicate with their loved ones who had crossed over into the next world. Mary was eager to believe in these mediums as it made her loss somewhat bearable, and she encouraged the president to attend a few séances, which he did. It is not clear if Lincoln participated to appease his wife or out of real interest and belief.

Q: Which president was the first to buy a car for the White House?

A: *William Howard Taft.* Taft knew that the United States was changing from an agrarian society to an industrial one, and he was open to the new technologies developing in the early twentieth century. So, in January 1909, the new president asked Congress for an appropriation to acquire automobiles for the White House. Congress authorized $12,000 for the purchase, and Taft selected a 40-horsepower White steam touring car and a 48-horsepower, 6-cylinder Pierce Arrow limousine.

Q: Which president had the greatest number of grandchildren?

A: *William Henry Harrison.* Harrison married Anna Tuthill Symmes on November 25, 1795, and together they had ten children, more than any president to that date. The president had the most grandchildren of any president—forty-eight. One of them—Benjamin Harrison—became the twenty-third president of the United States.

Souvenir wooden eggs from the White House Easter Egg Rolls: 1988 (Ronald Reagan), 1989 (George H. W. Bush), 1992 (Bill Clinton).

Q: Which first lady was the first to host the Easter Egg Roll at the White House?

A: *Lucy Hayes.* Easter eggs started rolling on the White House lawn in 1878, after Congress passed a law banning such activity on the Capitol grounds. Over the years, presidents have added personal touches to the festivities. First Lady Pat Nixon invited the Easter Bunny to join in. President Reagan hid autographed eggs for the kids to find. Hayes would probably be surprised to know that the White House Easter Egg Roll now spans eleven hours and accommodates more than thirty thousand children and their families.

Q: Which president had the first elevator installed in the White House?

A: *Chester Arthur.* Actually, James Garfield ordered a hydraulic elevator, but after Garfield was shot—and while he lay dying—the project was put on hold so as not to disturb the president. The elevator was eventually installed in the fall of 1881 during Arthur's administration.

Q: Which president called his wife "the boss"?

A: *Harry Truman.* Truman may have been kidding—or maybe not. Bess Truman had worked alongside her husband as a salesperson at the clothing store he co-owned, even before he entered politics. When he became a U.S. Senator, she worked in his office as a paid employee. Mrs. Truman was a no-nonsense type who disliked the fame thrust on her as first lady. She avoided social gatherings and press conferences and generally kept a low profile during her husband's administration.

Q: Who put solar panels on the White House roof?

A: *Jimmy Carter.* On June 20, 1979, the Carter administration installed thirty-two panels designed to harvest the sun's rays at the White House and use the resulting energy to heat water. But Carter's interest in solar technology was not shared by his successor, Ronald Reagan. Not only did the Reagan administration cut research and development budgets for renewable energy, but workers also quietly dismantled the White House solar panels in 1986, while resurfacing the roof. One of these panels now resides at the Smithsonian's National Museum of American History.

Q: Which president never lived in the White House?

A: *George Washington.* When Washington took the oath of office in 1789, there was not yet a capital city or a permanent residence for the chief executive. Washington lobbied to make Washington the capital (conveniently, he lived just across the Potomac River in Virginia) and hired James Hoban to design a home for the president. The house was not completed until 1800, three years after Washington retired and one year after his death.

Q: Which president was the first to invite an African American to dine at the White House?

A: *Theodore Roosevelt.* Roosevelt invited the famous African American educator Booker T. Washington to dine at the White House on October 16, 1901. Washington had been born into slavery but managed through great hardship to attend Hampton Institute and later become director of the Tuskegee Institute. He believed that education would give poor blacks an escape from sharecropping and debt.

Campaign button commemorating Washington's historic meal with Roosevelt, 1904.

Q: Which president had the first iron kitchen stove installed in the White House?

A: *Millard Fillmore.* The first iron cook stove was installed at the White House during Fillmore's administration. The White House staff resisted the new contraption and would not learn to use it. The president himself pitched in. He obtained drawings of the stove from the patent office and figured out how to operate its various drafts and pulleys.

Q: Which president was the first to have electricity in the White House?

A: *Benjamin Harrison.* Electricity came to the White House as part of a plan for wiring the State, War & Navy Building next door. The Edison Company installed a generator for both buildings and wires were strung across the White House lawn and under the conservatory. Wires were buried inside the plaster walls of the rooms and round switches were installed for turning the current on and off. President and Mrs. Harrison were so fearful of being shocked that they refused to touch the switches and called on the domestic staff to operate them.

Q: Who was the first president to be married while in office?

A: *John Tyler.* Tyler wasn't married at the White House, but he was the first president to marry while holding office. After the death of his first wife, Letitia, he became engaged and then married to twenty-four-year-old Julia Gardiner, who was his junior by thirty years. She loved the role of first lady so much that after leaving the White House she occasionally signed her letters, "Mrs. Ex-President Tyler."

Portrait of Julia Tyler, attributed to Cephus Giovanni Thompson, c. 1840.

Q: During which president's administration was almost the entire White House rebuilt?

A: *Harry Truman's.* Not long after Truman decided to add a balcony onto the South Portico of the White House, engineers found the entire mansion to be structurally unsound. The house was literally sagging under the weight of 150 years of use. Margaret Truman's piano leg broke through the floor and Truman's bathtub was sinking. A decision was made (with Congressional approval) to rebuild and update the historic structure from the inside out. The first family moved into Blair House across the street while the White House was under reconstruction.

Q: Which president was the first to install a telephone in the White House?

A: *Rutherford B. Hayes.* Hayes embraced Alexander Graham Bell's new invention and had a phone installed in the Executive Mansion. The president's phone number was "1."

Monroe china with border vignettes signifying strength, agriculture, commerce, art, and science, 1817.

Q: Which administration was the first to have official White House china?

A: *James Monroe's.* Before his administration, first families purchased china for their personal use and took it with them on leaving office. Monroe's White House china was created solely for official use by the president. It was manufactured by Dagoty-Honoré in Paris, France, in 1817. A dinner service of thirty place settings and a matching dessert service were purchased for $1,167.23. An eagle with a red, white, and blue banner reading E PLURIBUS UNUM decorates the center of each plate.

Chapter 7

First Families

WIVES, CHILDREN, AND PETS OF THE PRESIDENT

"I was an ordinary woman who was called onstage at an extraordinary time. I was no different once I became first lady than I had been before. But, through an accident of history, I had become interesting to people."

—*Betty Ford*

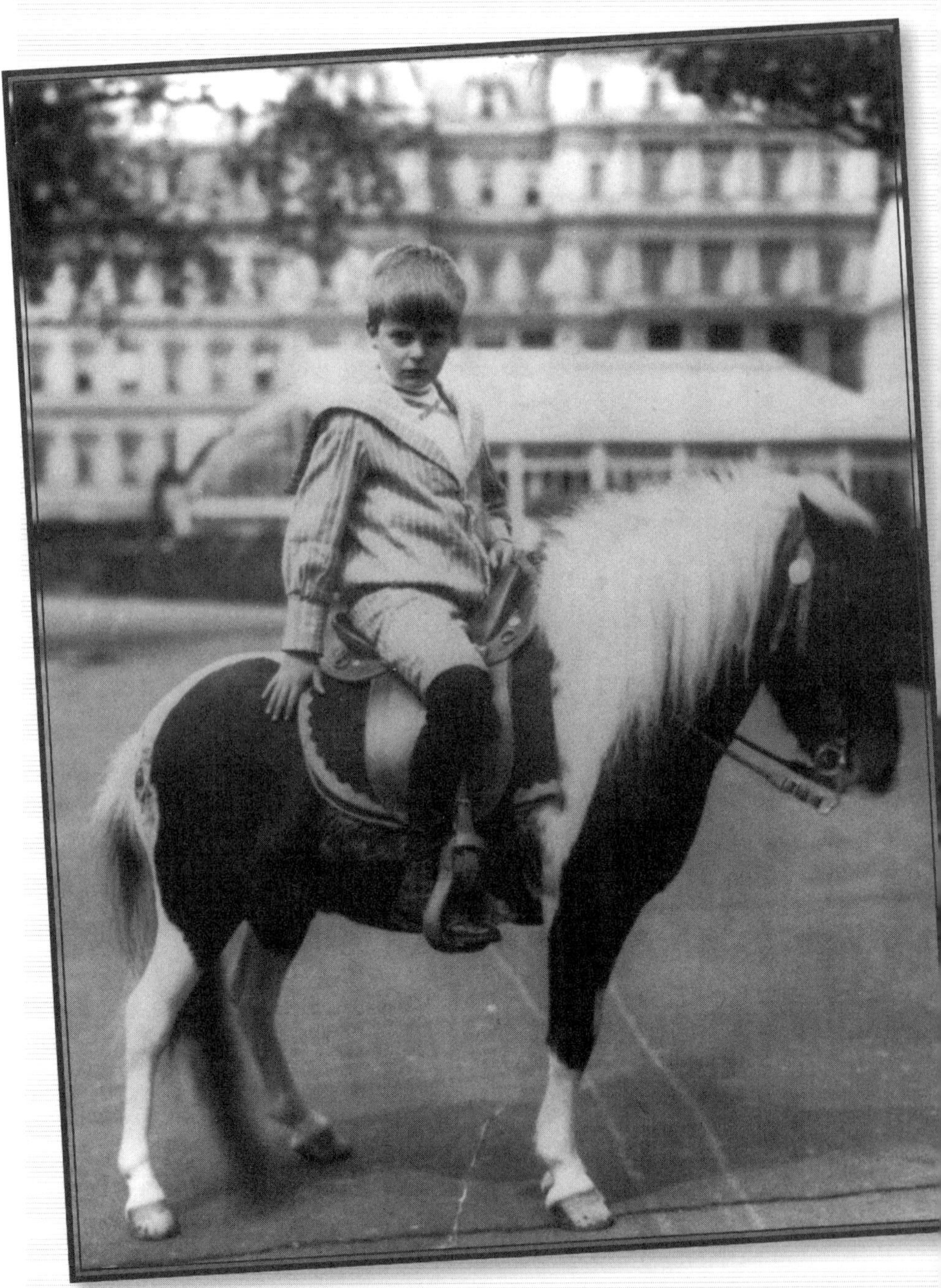

Archie Roosevelt with his beloved pony, Algonquin, June 17, 1902.

Q: Which president's children brought a pony upstairs in the White House elevator?

A: *Theodore Roosevelt's.* Roosevelt's wild sons and their friends became known as The White House Gang, and their shenanigans were an endless source of amusement to the public. Quentin Roosevelt made history by being the first first child to bring a horse upstairs in the White House. His brother Archie was sick in bed and Quentin thought that seeing his pony, Algonquin, would cheer him up.

Q: Which first lady wrote a book from her dog's point of view?

A: *Barbara Bush.* The Bushes' dog, Millie, was a popular White House pet. Mrs. Bush capitalized on her fame when writing *Millie's Book*, a Springer spaniel's view of the White House. The book became a best seller, and all proceeds went to literacy, which was a cause Mrs. Bush championed.

Q: Which first lady blamed her husband's involvement in politics for the death of their son?

A: *Jane Pierce.* Just two months before Franklin Pierce's inauguration, the Pierces' eleven-year-old son Benny died in a train accident, which plunged the president and first lady into mourning. Having already lost a son to typhus nine years earlier, the couple could barely control their grief. Jane gradually lost hold of reality and thought God was punishing them for Franklin's involvement in "dirty politics." She spent days in the White House writing tender notes to her deceased younger child.

Q: Which first lady's refusal to serve liquor in the White House made her a symbol for other reformers?

A: *Lucy Hayes.* Hayes was sometimes ridiculed for her belief in temperance and her refusal to serve alcohol in the White House, a practice that earned her the nickname Lemonade Lucy in later years. However, the first lady did not support the aggressive tactics of the Women's Christian Temperance Union, nor did she belong to it or any other temperance organization. Without becoming anyone's spokeswoman or ally, Hayes stuck to her guns. She was not the first woman to support a ban on liquor in the Executive Mansion. Sahara Sarah Polk, as she was known, was a deeply religious woman and did not serve alcohol or permit dancing or card playing.

Q: Who was the first woman to serve ice cream for dessert at the White House?

A: *Dolley Madison.* Thomas Jefferson brought the recipe for the new-fangled frozen dessert back from Europe and served it at the White House. Because Jefferson, a widower, had no one to act as hostess at official functions, Madison, the warm, effusive, and well-respected wife of James Madison, stepped up to the plate. She presided over many dinners and it was during one—or perhaps several—of these that she served ice cream. The novelty took off, and Dolley's name was forever after associated with the frozen treat.

Madison's presidential china, used officially after 1814, Nast Porcelain, Paris.

Q: Which first lady told her husband that if he became president she would "neither keep house nor make butter"?

A: *Sarah Polk.* Polk did the unthinkable for most women of her era—she voiced opinions. Having no children, and therefore few domestic responsibilities, Sarah became an unofficial adviser to her husband James, reading his speeches and discussing matters of state. Her power was not evident in public, but behind the scenes, she exerted more influence than most nineteenth-century first ladies.

Fan depicting the first eleven presidents, carried by Sarah Polk at her husband's inauguration, 1845.

Q: **Who was the first child of a president to be married in the White House?**

A: *Maria Monroe.* The younger daughter of James Monroe got married at the White House on March 9, 1820. Only family members attended and, much to the public's disappointment, there was little fanfare. Maria married her first cousin Samuel L. Gouverneur. The couple settled in New York City. Former president Monroe moved in with them after his wife died. President John Quincy Adams appointed Gouverneur postmaster of New York City.

Q: **Which first lady hired an astrologer to check the president's schedule?**

A: *Nancy Reagan.* The revelations about Mrs. Reagan's reliance on astrology were made in a book by ousted White House chief of staff Donald Regan. Mrs. Reagan admitted that after the attempted assassination of President Reagan in 1981, she turned to astrology for comfort. She arranged the president's daily schedule based on the advice of a San Francisco astrologer. Regan's characterization of Mrs. Reagan as a behind-the-scenes operator wielding undue influence over her husband's presidency was a blow to the first lady.

Q: Which first lady called the White House her "chilly castle"?

A: *Abigail Adams.* Adams was no wimp. She kept the family farm in Braintree, Massachusetts, from going under while her husband attended the Continental Congress during the American Revolution. So her complaint about the White House is probably no exaggeration—the cold, damp, unfinished Executive Mansion must have been less than welcoming when she arrived to become the first first lady to live there in 1800. Adams bemoaned her circumstances, "We have not the least fence, yard, or other convenience … and the great unfinished audience-room I make a drying-room of, to hang up the clothes in."

Engraving of Abigail Adams at age fifty-six, based on Gilbert Stuart's painting, c. 1800–15.

Q: Which first lady practiced early environmentalism in a project in the nation's capital called "beautification"?

A: *Lady Bird Johnson.* "Beautification" referred to a combination of rural and urban environmentalism, national parks conservation, anti-pollution measures, landscaping, and urban renewal. In 1965 Washington was a racially torn city with crumbling slums and devastating poverty. Mrs. Johnson raised funds to go into some of the tough neighborhoods and plant trees and flowers. She motivated local residents to bring positive changes to their dilapidated streets. Her efforts were a model for environmental efforts in the rest of the nation and soothed a city in turmoil over the civil rights movement and the Vietnam War.

Q: Who became the first African American first lady?

A: *Michelle Obama.* When her husband won the 2008 election, Obama made history as the first African American woman to be first lady. Born to a low-income family on Chicago's South Side, she attended Princeton University and earned a law degree from Harvard. She met Barack Obama while working at a law firm in Chicago, and they married in 1992. Mrs. Obama used her position to be a positive role model to young people and to work for social change.

Q: **Which first lady was married to her fifth cousin?**

A: *Eleanor Roosevelt.* Roosevelt married her dashing, distant cousin Franklin D. Roosevelt and became Anna Eleanor Roosevelt Roosevelt. When the two met, Eleanor was a shy young woman who volunteered as a social worker in New York's East Side slums, and Franklin was a sheltered student at Harvard. Franklin's mother opposed the match—and even took her son away on a cruise to separate the two—but they eventually tied the knot. Eleanor's uncle—President Theodore Roosevelt—gave away the bride.

Q: **Which first lady saved a French noblewoman's life?**

A: *Elizabeth Monroe.* Monroe was in France while her husband James served as U.S. minister there just after the French Revolution. When James learned that the family of the Marquis de Lafayette was imprisoned for their supposed loyalty to the King, he felt helpless. The Marquis had aided Washington's army during the Revolutionary War but as an American diplomat, Monroe felt he could not interfere. Instead he asked Elizabeth to go visit Madame de Lafayette, who had received a death sentence. News of Elizabeth's visit spread throughout Paris, and the noblewoman was spared execution and soon released.

Q: Who was the first child born at the White House?

A: *James Madison Randolph.* A grandson of Thomas Jefferson, he was born in the White House in January 1806, the eighth child of Jefferson's older daughter, Martha Jefferson Randolph. The first girl born in the White House was Mary Louisa Adams, granddaughter of John Quincy Adams. She was born on December 2, 1828.

Mary Louisa Adams' doll Sally, c. 1829.

Grace Coolidge with Rebecca, one of her many White House pets, 1927.

Q: Which first lady kept a pet raccoon at the White House?

A: *Grace Coolidge.* Coolidge's pet raccoon, Rebecca, delighted children at the White House Easter Egg Roll in 1927. Rebecca reportedly had her own little house, built by the president himself. In addition to Rebecca and a variety of other pets, the Coolidges had beautiful white collies named Rob Roy and Prudence Prim. Rob Roy appears in an official White House portrait of Mrs. Coolidge, painted by Howard Chandler Christy.

Q: Who was the first president to have a pet cat?

A: *Abraham Lincoln.* Lincoln loved kittens and was allegedly the first president to have a cat in the White House. Called Tabby, the "first cat" may have inspired one of the president's sayings: "No matter how much cats fight, there always seem to be plenty of kittens."

Which first lady saved a portrait of George Washington from a White House fire?

Dolley Madison. During the War of 1812, British troops invaded the city of Washington. At the White House, Madison had to make a critical decision. Her husband was not at home, and there was little time to evacuate before the invading forces arrived. While various sources have expressed skepticism about her account recorded several years later, Mrs. Madison's story is that she packed up her husband's papers and the national seal, and ordered that the large portrait of George Washington be taken down from the wall, stripped of its frame, and loaded onto a cart. Once these national treasures were safe, she left the mansion. When she and James Madison returned to the White House three days later, their home was a burned-out shell.

Q:

Which first lady was the first to put up a Christmas tree in the White House?

A:

Caroline Harrison. Even though her sister died in early December 1889 in the White House, Caroline still went ahead with her plans for the first Christmas tree in the White House's history. Decorating Christmas trees at the White House has been a tradition ever since.

Q: Which first lady was the first to hold a college degree?

A: *Lucy Hayes.* In June 1850, Lucy Webb graduated from Wesleyan Female College in Cincinnati, Ohio. She had not yet turned twenty. Although her education conferred on her the status of "new woman," it did not grant her a wide range of options in society. After marrying Rutherford B. Hayes, she dutifully took on the roles of wife and mother. She remained a woman of high morals and strong views, which made her both adored and reviled as first lady.

Lucy Hayes, photo by C. M. Bell, 1877.

Q: Which first lady was an actress before marrying?

A: *Nancy Reagan.* After college, Nancy Davis was a sales clerk at Marshall Fields department store and a nurse's aide in Chicago, but she soon landed a non-speaking part in a play that eventually came to Broadway. She lived and acted in New York until 1949, when she had a successful screen test and was offered a seven-year contract with Metro Goldwyn Mayer in Hollywood. She made eleven feature films with MGM, including one—*Hellcats of the Navy*—in which she appeared with her husband, Ronald Reagan.

Q: Which twentieth-century first lady never gave an interview during her husband's time in the White House?

A: *Bess Truman.* Bess never even wanted Harry to be vice president, so when he became president she was resentful and unhappy. It showed in her actions as first lady. She discontinued the first lady press conferences established by her predecessor, Eleanor Roosevelt, and entertained as little as possible. This may have been due, in part, to the fact that the White House was under repair for much of Truman's time in office.

Q: Which first lady shocked the nation by her outspoken support of the Equal Rights Amendment?

A: *Betty Ford.* Ford actively lobbied for passage of the Equal Rights Amendment (ERA). The first lady knew that no amendment would be a quick fix toward putting women on equal footing with men, but she thought it might "help knock down those restrictions that have locked women into old stereotypes of behavior." Ford hosted meetings in which federal commissions discussed the status of women and was instrumental in her husband's executive order that created a national commission to coordinate American efforts in conjunction with the United Nation's International Women's Year in 1975. Her candid discussion of women's issues—from raising children to battling breast cancer—earned her enormous respect from the American public.

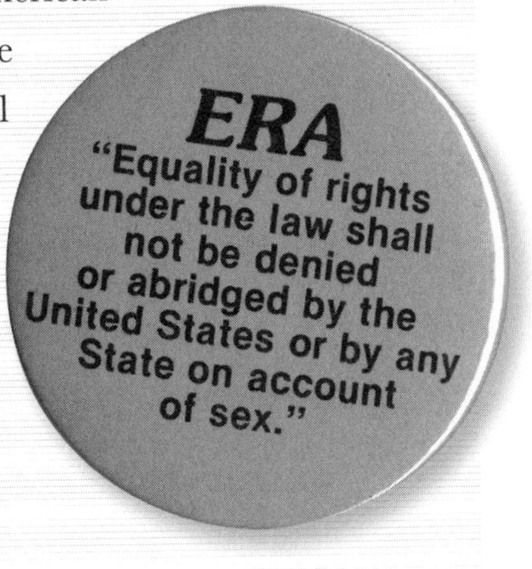

ERA
"Equality of rights under the law shall not be denied or abridged by the United States or by any State on account of sex."

ERA button with the language of the proposed amendment, c. 1970s.

Q: Which first lady ran for political office while in the White House?

A: *Hillary Clinton.* After a high-profile campaign, during which her husband Bill stumped for her, Clinton was elected U.S. senator from New York in 2000. As senator, Clinton forged relationships with both Republicans and Democrats. She served on the Budget, Armed Services, and Health, Education, Labor and Pension committees.

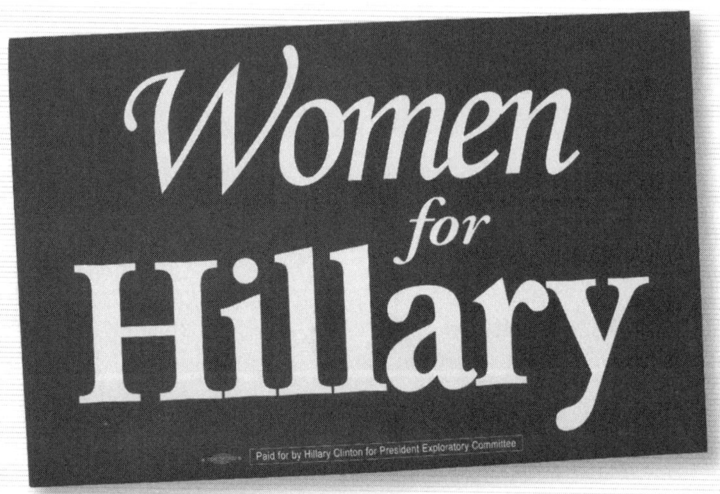

Poster from Hillary Clinton's presidential campaign, 2008.

Q: Which president's daughter was known to carry a live snake in her purse?

A: *Theodore Roosevelt's daughter Alice.* A born rebel, Alice was famous for her high spirits and biting wit. She smoked in public and created a scandal by carrying a live snake in her purse. Her antics prompted Roosevelt to remark, "I can either run the country or I can attend to Alice, but I cannot possibly do both." Alice married Republican Congressman Nicholas Longworth of Ohio. After his death in 1931, she remained in the capital and was referred to as "the other Washington monument."

Q: Which first lady was a librarian?

A: *Laura Bush.* Before her marriage, Mrs. Bush earned a degree in library science and worked as a librarian. As first lady, her love of books and reading prompted her to host the first National Book Festival at the Library of Congress in the fall of 2001. She was always a passionate reader. As first lady of Texas, when her husband was governor, she founded the Texas Book Festival. She is also a published author.

Q: Which president's dog had his initials?

A: *Lyndon Baines Johnson's Little Beagle Johnson.* Most families have some kind of tradition, and in Johnson's family, everyone had to have the same initials—even the dog. While in the Senate, Johnson had a pup he called Little Beagle Johnson. LBJ's daughters were named Luci Baines Johnson and Lynda Bird Johnson, and his wife, whose real name was Claudia, was called Lady Bird.

Q: Who was the first first lady to hold a job before marriage?

A: *Abigail Fillmore.* For most of her twenties Fillmore was a teacher. She gave up her career after the birth of her first child in 1828. Her education made her an asset to the president because she understood the issues of the time, and she was supportive of Fillmore's rise in politics. Despite health problems that kept her from being a fully active first lady, Mrs. Fillmore made a lasting contribution by establishing a library in the White House.

LBJ with Little Beagle Johnson, photo by Thomas D. McAvoy, 1960.

Q: Who was the first woman to have both a husband and son serve as president?

A: *Abigail Adams.* Abigail's husband, John Adams, was president from 1797 to 1801. Her son John Quincy Adams served from 1825 to 1829. History repeats itself—once anyway. In 1988, George H. W. Bush was elected to the top office. His son George W. Bush became president in 2000, making Barbara Bush the second woman to have both a husband and a son lead the country.

Q: Who was the first first lady to hold a graduate degree?

A: *Pat Nixon.* Nixon attended four years of college at the University of Southern California and graduated with the equivalent of a master's degree. She became a teacher and continued to teach for the first year of her marriage. She is also credited with being the first wife of a president to wear pants in public.

Q: **Which first lady called the White House "that dull and stately prison"?**

A: *Louisa Adams.* The wife of John Quincy Adams had been an accomplished musician before becoming first lady and often gave performances for friends and guests. After moving into the White House, she became reclusive and depressed. At the White House, Louisa felt isolated from the city of Washington and considered the living conditions in the mansion deplorable.

Standing harp belonging to Louisa Adams, c. 1820s.

Q: Which first lady descended into a silver mine reportedly because her husband bet she'd be too afraid to go?

A: *Julia Grant.* The spirited first lady picked up a miner's lamp and ventured into the so-called Big Bonanza silver mine in Nevada. Having endured long separations from her husband as a military wife, she was used to toughing it out. Despite the many scandals that plagued Grant's administration, she blossomed in the White House and called it "quite the happiest period of my life."

Julia Grant, accompanied by Ulysses, visits the Virginia City mine, 1879.

Q: Who was the first wife of a president to be able to vote for her husband?

A: *Florence Harding.* Florence supported women's suffrage and she supported her husband, unofficially conducting his presidential campaign. She must have been very happy that the Nineteenth Amendment giving women the right to vote passed in time for the 1920 election. It enabled her to do what no first lady before her could: cast a ballot for her husband.

Q: Which first lady caused a "fist-bump frenzy"?

A: *Michelle Obama.* It was called the "first bump heard 'round the world" by *The Washington Post.* On June 3, 2008, when Mrs. Obama fist-bumped her husband after a speech in which he declared victory in the Democratic primaries, the focus shifted from his election to her assertive action. The press had a field day with it. Was it a "black" culture thing? An expression of affection? A "gimme-five" type deal? Or even a terrorist fist jab? Ultimately, the candidate himself weighed in, telling a reporter it "captured what I love about my wife—there's an irreverence about her and a sense that for all the hoopla, that I'm her husband and sometimes we'll do silly things."

Q: **The children of which two presidents have written murder mysteries about Washington, D.C.?**

A: *Elliot Roosevelt, son of Franklin D. Roosevelt, and Margaret Truman, daughter of Harry Truman.* Washington was definitely an inspiration—even if a grisly one—for these first children. In Roosevelt's books, his mother, Eleanor, is the protagonist whom he casts as an amateur detective. Truman uses Washington as a backdrop for her mysteries. Her murders have been set in the Capitol, the White House, and at the Smithsonian.

Q: **Who was the first first lady to have an office in the West Wing?**

A: *Hillary Clinton.* When she set up shop in the West Wing of the White House alongside the President's senior staff, Mrs. Clinton broke the mold for first ladies. Until then, first ladies customarily operated from the East Wing of the White House, away from the president's top advisers. At the urging of her husband, Clinton helped formulate policy on health care and other domestic issues.

Q: Which first lady was an advocate for and national president of the Girl Scouts of America?

A: *Lou Hoover.* Hoover had served as national president of the Girl Scouts of America before entering the White House. As first lady she became the organization's honorary national president. A well-educated woman with diverse interests that ranged from taxidermy to Chinese, she felt that the Girl Scouts promoted active, self-reliant young ladies who had high self-esteem and took on leadership roles in their communities.

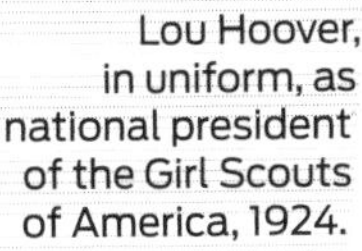

Lou Hoover, in uniform, as national president of the Girl Scouts of America, 1924.

Q: Which president's wife was the first to be officially and nationally recognized as "first lady"?

A: *Lucy Hayes.* Martha Washington was called Lady Washington for want of a better title. In fact, there was no permanent title for the first lady until Hayes's tenure began in 1877. But even before Hayes, "first lady" was given a trial run. At Dolley Madison's funeral in 1849, Zachary Taylor eulogized her as "the first lady of the land" and there is at least one written instance of Mary Todd Lincoln being referred to as first lady as well, though the term was still little used. The phrase was also used to describe Harriet Lane, James Buchanan's niece who served as his hostess from 1857 to 1861. Not knowing how one should refer to a non-spouse, the press often referred to Harriet as "first lady of the White House."

Chapter 8

Impeachment, Controversy, Shame

LOW MOMENTS IN THE NATION'S HIGHEST OFFICE

"I am not a crook."

—*Richard Nixon*

Q: Which president shot and killed a man?

A: *Andrew Jackson.* On May 30, 1806, future president Andrew Jackson shot and killed Charles Dickinson in a duel. Jackson and Dickinson, both Tennessee plantation owners, had argued about a horse-racing bet. The argument became very public, with Dickinson eventually insulting Jackson's wife, Rachel. Exploding with anger, Jackson challenged Dickinson to a duel. Although Jackson was wounded, he proved the better shot. Death by duel was not considered a crime in those days, and Jackson went on to have a successful career in politics.

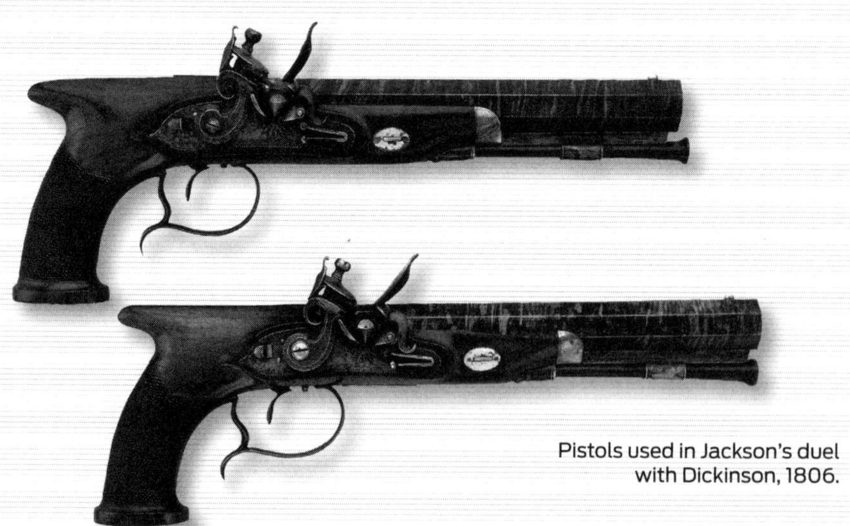

Pistols used in Jackson's duel with Dickinson, 1806.

Q: Which president secretly had surgery to protect the public from news of his illness?

A: *Grover Cleveland.* When doctors discovered a cancerous growth on the roof of Cleveland's mouth in 1893, they decided to operate immediately. But White House aides feared that if Americans thought their president was at risk there would be mass hysteria. The public was informed that the president was embarking on a pleasure cruise. Once aboard the yacht, however, his doctors took over, gave him an anesthetic, and performed surgery that cost him about five teeth and a significant piece of his upper left jawbone. He was taken to Cape Cod for recovery and was back in the Oval Office before too long. Twenty-four years later, the truth of Cleveland's surgery was revealed.

Q: Which first lady was accused of being a spy?

A: *Mary Lincoln.* Three of Mrs. Lincoln's half-brothers died in Confederate military service during the Civil War: Sam at Shiloh; David, after wounds sustained at Vicksburg; and Alexander at Baton Rouge. She did not openly mourn them, however, because she was a firm supporter of the Union cause. Mrs. Lincoln showed her devotion to the Union by holding events for Union soldiers at the White House and visiting injured Union troops in military hospitals. Southerners condemned her as an enemy, and the fact that she had Confederate relatives led northerners to accuse her of being a spy.

Q: Who is the only president to commit a public act of treason against the U.S. government?

A: *John Tyler.* As president in the early 1840s, Tyler, who was a native Virginian, supported many policies his party did not—states rights and slavery, to name two. Sixteen years after leaving office, when Civil War seemed inevitable, Tyler chaired a peace conference between representatives from the North and South with the goal of keeping the Union intact. When the peace efforts he spearheaded failed, Tyler embraced the Confederacy and urged fellow Virginians to join him. He was eventually elected to the Confederate Congress, which was officially at war with the country he once served.

Q: Who were the only presidents to be impeached?

A: *Andrew Johnson and Bill Clinton.* Johnson, who became president in 1865, showed leniency to the Southern states in the wake of their defeat in the Civil War—so much so that he came under fire by a group of congressmen called the Radical Republicans. When Johnson would not yield to their demands, they called for his impeachment. He was saved from being removed from office by just one vote in the Senate. More than a century later, Clinton suffered the same indignity when he lied about his "inappropriate relationship" with a twenty-two-year-old White House intern. Impeachment charges of perjury and obstruction of justice threatened to end his presidency, but though impeached by the House, he was easily acquitted in the Senate, with voting in both houses following largely partisan lines.

U.S. Senate gallery tickets for impeachment trials of Johnson (1868) and Clinton (1999).

Q: Who was the only president to resign?

A: *Richard Nixon.* In June 1972, five "burglars" were caught attempting to bug the Democratic Party headquarters at the Watergate complex in Washington, D.C. It was rumored that the Republican president knew of the crime and was behind the break-in, but Nixon denied any wrongdoing. However, during the investigation into the Watergate affair, witnesses confirmed that Nixon had directed a cover-up and there were tapes of conversations held in the Oval Office to prove it. Nixon resigned in order to avoid the impeachment process.

Earphones and listening station used in the Nixon impeachment inquiry, 1974.

Q: **Which first lady was accused of poisoning her husband?**

A: *Florence Harding.* Warren Harding was on a cross-country trip when he became ill. He died suddenly on August 2, 1923, in San Francisco. His wife was the last person to see him alive. In 1930 Gaston Means published a book called *The Strange Death of President Harding*, in which he accused Mrs. Harding of killing her husband, perhaps in retaliation for Harding's well-known affairs with other women. Means had no proof, but his sensational claims caused quite a stir. Although Mrs. Harding would not permit an autopsy of her husband, historians widely discount Gaston's story and believe that Harding died of natural causes.

Q: Which first lady sparked a scandal by modeling for an advertisement?

A: *Julia Tyler.* The second wife of John Tyler was a charming twenty-four-year-old when they married, but only a few years earlier her parents had fought frantically to control her tainted image. The vivacious Julia, then only nineteen years of age, had modeled for an advertisement for a dry goods and clothing emporium. Her little commercial venture caused an unwanted stir. The girl known as the Rose of Long Island was whisked off to Europe. She later landed in Washington, D.C., where she met her future husband.

"Scandalous" advertisement featuring the future Mrs. Tyler, c. 1839.

Q: Which president was accused of fathering an illegitimate child?

A: *Grover Cleveland.* In 1874, Maria C. Halpin gave birth to a baby boy and identified Cleveland as the child's father. Cleveland acknowledged the brief affair, but he was not entirely sure the child was his. Despite the uncertainty, Cleveland and his supporters claimed that he did the honorable thing and paid child support to Halpin. During the campaign of 1884 the story of Halpin and Cleveland's illegitimate son came back to haunt the candidate. Cleveland's detractors taunted, "Ma, Ma, where's my Pa? Gone to the White House, Ha, Ha, Ha!" But Cleveland confronted the matter head on—he candidly admitted having the affair and supporting Halpin's son—and won the election.

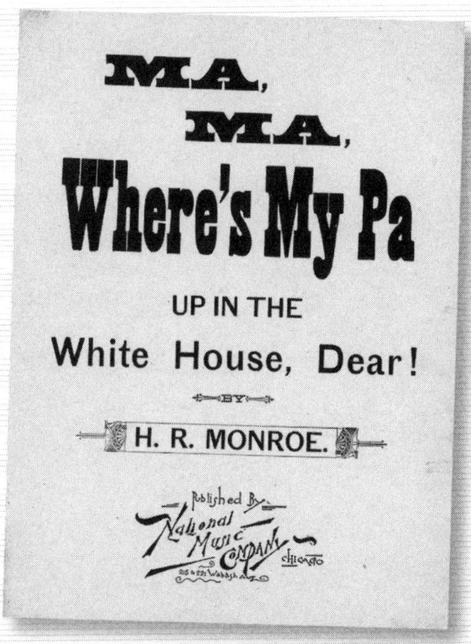

Scandal-inspired anti-Cleveland campaign music, by H. R. Monroe, 1884.

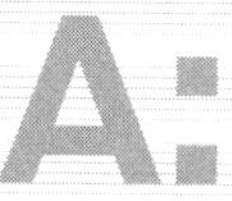

Which president pardoned another president for any illegal activities he may have committed while in office?

A: *Gerald Ford.* On September 8, 1974, Gerald Ford, who became president after Richard Nixon resigned in the wake of the Watergate scandal, pardoned his predecessor, declaring, "My conscience tells me clearly and certainly that I cannot prolong the bad dreams that continue to reopen a chapter that is closed. My conscience tells me that only I, as President, have the constitutional power to firmly shut and seal this book. My conscience tells me it is my duty, not merely to proclaim domestic tranquility but to use every means that I have to insure it." However, Ford's attempt to heal the country after Watergate was denounced by many Americans who thought Nixon should be tried for his crimes and who felt that Ford's pardon represented payback for Nixon's appointment of Ford to the vice presidency the year before.

Q: Which first lady caused a "china scandal"?

A: *Nancy Reagan.* As the Reagan Administration was cutting programs for the poor, the first lady was ordering a new set of White House china for $200,000. Mrs. Reagan was widely criticized for her extravagance despite the fact that the china was purchased by a private donor and not with government funds.

Reagan White House china manufactured by Lenox in 1981.

Q: Which president allegedly was given a speeding ticket?

A: *Ulysses S. Grant.* The former general loved to ride—and he loved to ride fast. Grant brought his favorite horses with him to the White House and enjoyed taking a spin in the capital city. On one particular night, according to a popular story, Grant's horse-drawn buggy came careening down a street right past a police officer. The officer caught up to the reckless driver and cited him for excessive speed. But as he was writing the ticket, it dawned on him that the violator was none other than the president. Despite the officer's apologies, according to the story, Grant insisted on paying the twenty-dollar fine.

Q: Which first lady's excessive spending in the White House caused political trouble for her husband?

A: *Mary Lincoln.* Mrs. Lincoln, already temperamental and emotionally fragile as a young woman, grew more so in the White House. As first lady she went on unchecked spending sprees, which by 1864 had produced a debt of $27,000. She overspent her budget when redecorating the White House and bought three hundred pairs of gloves in a four-month period. Mary's suspect accounting practices and her acceptance of gifts from those who wanted to curry favor with her husband caused great political embarrassment for the president.

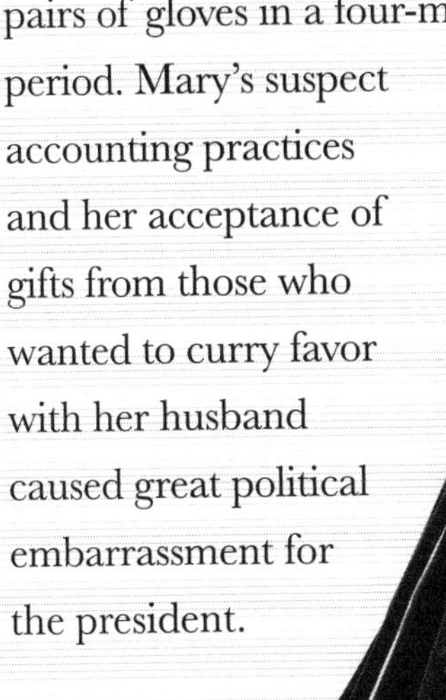

Purple velvet skirt with daytime bodice, worn by Mary Lincoln during the Washington season, 1861–62.

Q: **Which first lady was accused of bigamy?**

A: *Rachel Jackson.* Rachel, wife of Andrew Jackson, had been married previously to Lewis Robards, an abusive husband who eventually threw her out of the house. The two were later divorced—or so she thought. She married the future president in 1791, only to discover the terrible truth—she was still legally tied to Robards. The situation was corrected in 1794, but Jackson's opponents in the 1828 election hoped to discredit him by circulating rumors that Mrs. Jackson was a bigamist.

Chapter 9

Assassination, Death, and National Mourning

FROM MARTYRS TO MEMORIALS

"It takes more than that to kill a bull moose."

—*Theodore Roosevelt in a 1912 campaign address, after having survived an assassination attempt*

Q: What were the first presidential items given to the Smithsonian?

A: *The top hat worn by Abraham Lincoln and the chair he sat in at Ford's Theatre on the evening of his assassination.* Both were brought to the Smithsonian in 1867, after the conspirators in the president's death were tried and hanged. Officials from the War Department had recovered the items from the presidential box shortly after John Wilkes Booth shot Lincoln on April 14, 1865. Although the chair was later given to the descendants of the owners of Ford's Theatre, the hat may still be seen at the Smithsonian, along with other treasures that commemorate the life and death of the sixteenth president.

Lincoln's top hat, last worn on the evening of his assassination, April 14, 1865.

Q: **How many presidents have died while serving in office?**

A: *Eight.* They are William Henry Harrison, Zachary Taylor, Abraham Lincoln, James Garfield, William McKinley, Warren Harding, Franklin D. Roosevelt, and John F. Kennedy. Of those, four were assassinated—Lincoln, Garfield, McKinley, and Kennedy.

Q: **Which three presidents died on July 4?**

A: *John Adams, Thomas Jefferson, and James Monroe.* Adams and Jefferson actually died on the same day—July 4, 1826, the fiftieth anniversary of the adoption of the Declaration of Independence. Monroe died on July 4, 1831. According to Jefferson's physician, the former president lay in a semi-conscious state at Monticello for the last few days of his life, rousing himself once to ask, "Is it the Fourth?" At the same time Adams was languishing in his bed in Massachusetts. On July 4, it is said that he rallied for a moment and uttered, "Thomas Jefferson still survives," not knowing that Jefferson had, in fact, expired only hours before.

Q: Which president's assassination was called the end of Camelot?

A: *John F. Kennedy's.* JFK's administration became associated with the image of King Arthur's court when Mrs. Kennedy mentioned, in an interview after her husband's death, that the title song to the popular Broadway musical, *Camelot*, had been one of her husband's favorites. The song refers to "one brief shining moment" in the kingdom, which many came to identify with the glamorous and all-too-short Kennedy administration. Kennedy's youth and style had all the romance and charm of the mythical kingdom.

One of four drums played during Kennedy's funeral procession, November 1963.

Q: Which president died suddenly while the country was at war?

A: *Franklin D. Roosevelt.* FDR died on April 12, 1945, of a cerebral hemorrhage, while the country was still engaged in World War II. Vice President Harry Truman was summoned immediately. When Mrs. Roosevelt told him the president had died, he asked her, "Is there anything I can do for you?" Mrs. Roosevelt replied, "Is there anything we can do for *you*? For you are the one in trouble now."

Song lamenting Roosevelt's death, by Tommy McWilliams and Lou Zoeller, 1945.

Q: **Which president's son was present or nearby when three presidential assassinations took place?**

A: *Abraham Lincoln's son Robert.* Robert was quickly called to his father's deathbed after the president was shot at Ford's Theater, and was on the scene shortly after the assassinations of James Garfield and William McKinley. On July 2, 1881, Lincoln, who served as secretary of war to Garfield, arrived at the Baltimore & Potomac train station only to learn that Garfield had just been shot. Lincoln rushed to his aid. Twenty years later, Lincoln was on his way to the Pan-American Exposition in Buffalo when he was informed that McKinley had been shot. He hurried to visit the stricken president. All three presidents died after seeing Robert, though in Garfield's case, it took him more than two months to do so.

Q: **Which former president suffered a fatal stroke in the U.S. House of Representatives?**

A: *John Quincy Adams.* Adams, who represented Massachusetts as a congressman after his retirement from the presidency, had just cast a vote on the House floor when he suffered a massive stroke. He was carried to the Speaker's Room and died two days later on February 23, 1848. The eighty-year-old statesman lay in state in a House committee room, where mourners filed by his open casket.

Q: Who was the first president to be assassinated?

A: *Abraham Lincoln.* The leader of the Union was attacked by actor John Wilkes Booth, a Southern sympathizer, at Ford's Theatre in Washington, D.C., on April 14, 1865. The president had been enjoying a performance of *Our American Cousin* when Booth entered the presidential box and shot him. Witnesses claimed that Booth cried, "*Sic semper tyrannis!*" (Thus always to tyrants!) as he leapt from the box to the stage and made his getaway. The wounded president was taken to a house across the street from the theater, where he died the next morning.

Q: Which president was saved from two assassination attempts?

Gerald Ford. Ford had the misfortune to experience two assassination attempts in 1975. On September 5, Lynette "Squeaky" Fromme, who had been a follower of mass murderer Charles Manson, took aim at Ford as he shook hands with supporters outside the Senator Hotel in Sacramento, California. An alert Secret Service agent grabbed the gun to prevent it from firing and Fromme was immediately apprehended. Later that month, on September 22, political activist Sara Jane Moore fired on Ford from forty feet away but missed. Both women were given life sentences for their crimes, though later paroled. Ford was not hurt in either incident.

Q: Who became the first first lady to attend her assassinated husband's funeral?

A: *Lucretia Garfield.* In July 1881, Mrs. Garfield was shocked to receive a telegram informing her that her husband—who had only been in office a few months—had been shot. She was recuperating from a serious bout of malaria at the New Jersey shore, but rushed back to Washington to be with him. In early September, the two went back to the shore, as it was believed that exposure to the sea air would hasten the recovery of the seriously wounded president. But Garfield died on September 19, 1881. Mrs. Garfield arranged for and attended the funeral, unlike Mary Lincoln, who was too distraught to attend Lincoln's.

Garfield mourning ribbon, 1881.

Q: Which president wrote his own epitaph?

A: *Thomas Jefferson.* The Sage of Monticello was a skilled writer—even when it came to composing the epitaph for his tombstone. It was a modest statement:

HERE WAS BURIED
THOMAS JEFFERSON
AUTHOR OF THE
DECLARATION
OF
AMERICAN INDEPENDENCE
OF THE
STATUTE OF VIRGINIA
FOR
RELIGIOUS FREEDOM
AND FATHER OF THE
UNIVERSITY OF VIRGINIA
BORN APRIL 2, 1743 O.S.
DIED JULY 4. 1826

Notice that he omitted the fact that he served as the third president of the United States from 1801 to 1809.

Q: The following men were pallbearers at which president's funeral: Robert Lincoln (son of President Abraham Lincoln), Philip Sheridan (Civil War general), Charles Lewis Tiffany (Tiffany & Co. founder), and Cornelius Vanderbilt (railroad mogul)?

A: *Chester Arthur.* Arthur, known for his good cheer and extensive wardrobe, died of complications from Bright's disease on November 18, 1886, at his home in New York City. His funeral took place at the Church of the Heavenly Rest in Manhattan. The impressive list of pallbearers reflects Arthur's strong connections to those with wealth, fame, and political power.

Q: Which two presidents are buried in Arlington National Cemetery in Virginia?

A: *William Howard Taft and John F. Kennedy.* Veterans and military personnel of every war from the Civil War to military operations in Iraq and Afghanistan are interred at Arlington Cemetery in Virginia, which was formerly the estate of Confederate general Robert E. Lee's wife, Mary Custis Lee. Before he was president, Taft served as secretary of war from 1904 to 1908. Kennedy was commander of a PT boat in World War II. An eternal flame burns at his grave.

Q: Which president died from an assassin's bullet after more than a dozen doctors failed to heal him?

A: *James Garfield.* Garfield was shot twice by Charles Guiteau, a disappointed office seeker, on July 2, 1881. One bullet merely grazed him, but the other shot lodged in his lower back. A team of surgeons treated the president, who endured three operations, none of which successfully extracted the bullet. Throughout the summer more doctors were brought in to assist. Inventor Alexander Graham Bell even employed his innovative "induction balance"—a type of metal detector—to find the bullet, but failed. In probing the wound—often with unsterilized fingers and instruments—these experts did more harm than good. Garfield died of blood poisoning on September 19, 1881.

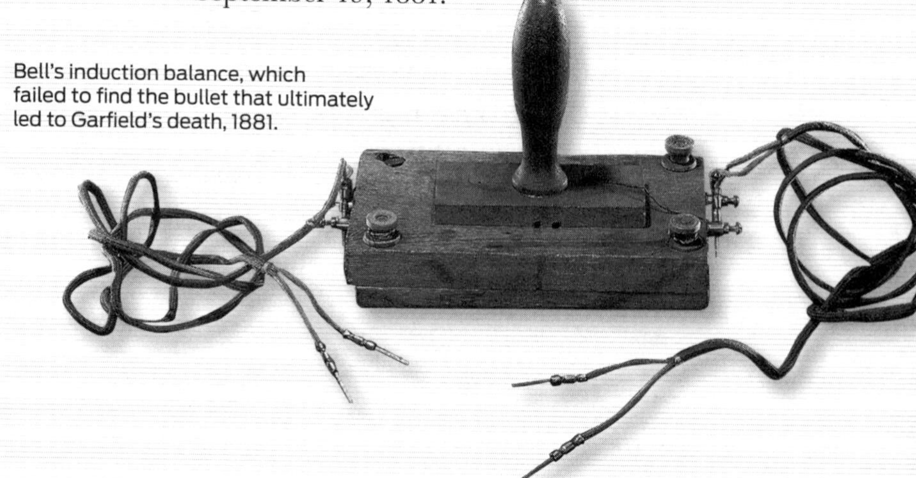

Bell's induction balance, which failed to find the bullet that ultimately led to Garfield's death, 1881.

Q: What was the first presidential funeral broadcast on radio?

A: *William Howard Taft's.* Ex-president Taft served as chief justice of the Supreme Court until a few weeks before his death on March 8, 1930. A military procession escorted Taft's coffin from his home, past the White House to the Capitol, where he lay in state. A service was then held at a nearby church, where a radio microphone was hidden among the flowers so the funeral service could be broadcast to listeners throughout the country.

Q: Which president died with Confederate money in his pocket?

A: *Abraham Lincoln.* When Lincoln was shot at Ford's Theatre in Washington, D.C., on April 14, 1865, he was carrying two pairs of spectacles, a lens polisher, pocketknife, watch fob, linen handkerchief, brown leather wallet containing a five-dollar Confederate note, and nine newspaper clippings. These everyday items were given to his son Robert on Lincoln's death. Why a Confederate note on the Union president? Some think it may have been a souvenir, picked up by Lincoln when he traveled to Virginia the week before, after the fall of Richmond.

Q: **Which former president was saved from an assassin's bullet by a speech tucked into his breast pocket?**

A: *Theodore Roosevelt.* Having already served nearly two full terms, from 1901to 1909, Roosevelt ran for president again in 1912, as a candidate for the Progressive Party, popularly known as the Bull Moose Party. He was en route to give a campaign speech at Milwaukee Auditorium on October 14, 1912, when John Schrank—who mistakenly believed that Roosevelt had been responsible for the assassination of William McKinley—fired on him. The bullet was deflected by Roosevelt's metal eyeglass case and a folded 50-page speech. When he delivered his address shortly thereafter, Roosevelt, only slightly wounded, held the bullet-ridden speech aloft for the audience to see.

Page of Roosevelt's speech pierced by a bullet, October 14, 1912.

-1-

Under these circumstances, it has been a matter of genuine regret to me that Senator LaFollette, who has done so much for the Progressive Cause, has felt that because of his antagonism to me he was obliged to range himself against the Progressive Movement in this campaign, thereby giving to his old-time enemies, the reactionaries, a much needed support which they have acknowledged by the first praise they have given him in twenty years. It has been asserted that I did not take sides with the LaFollette people in their campaign in Wisconsin in 1904. This is an error. On October 16th, of that year, I made my position clear in a letter to Mr. Cortelyou, Chairman of the National Republican Committee, which ran in part as follows:

> "I think Babcock and hi[illegible]ple should be told that, especially in vie[illegible] of the decision of the Supreme Court, there must not be any kind

Q: **Which president was the target of the first assassination attempt on a chief executive?**

A: *Andrew Jackson.* On January 30, 1835, Jackson attended a congressional funeral in the Capitol building. As he exited, Richard Lawrence, an unemployed house painter, attempted to fire his pistol at Jackson. The weapon failed to discharge, and the sixty-seven-year-old president escaped unharmed. Lawrence, who harbored a wide array of delusions, believed Jackson had conspired to keep him poor and out of work. Jackson was convinced that Lawrence was a Whig hit man who was trying to stop his plan to destroy the Bank of the United States. Lawrence spent the rest of his life in jails and asylums.

Q: **How many presidents have lain in state in the Rotunda of the U.S. Capitol?**

A: *Eleven.* They are Abraham Lincoln, James Garfield, William McKinley, Warren Harding, William Howard Taft, John F. Kennedy, Dwight Eisenhower, Herbert Hoover, Lyndon Johnson, Ronald Reagan, and Gerald Ford. Since its completion in 1824, the Rotunda of the United States Capitol has been considered the most suitable place for the nation to pay final tribute to its most eminent citizens by having their remains lie in state. These occasions are either authorized by a congressional resolution or approved by the congressional leadership.

Q: After he was wounded by an assassin's bullet, which president said, "I forgot to duck"?

A: *Ronald Reagan.* On March 30, 1981, as Reagan left the Washington Hilton Hotel, John Hinckley Jr. fired six shots at the president in just thirty seconds. The final bullet entered Reagan's left side and lodged about an inch from his heart. The first bullet hit press secretary James Brady in the head. Secret Service agents pushed Reagan into his limousine and rushed him to George Washington University Hospital. Weak from blood loss, Reagan still managed one of his trademark quips, when he said, "I forgot to duck," as doctors prepared him for surgery. He made a complete recovery, but Brady's serious injuries helped spur a nationwide push for stricter gun control.

Q: Which president owned a ring that contained a piece of George Washington's coffin?

A: *Abraham Lincoln.* The ring, fashioned by a Scottish jeweler, had a bust of Washington on the face. When one lifted the hinged top, a fragment of Washington's rosewood coffin was in glass below. There were thirteen tiny gold stars embedded in the splinter. A man named Mr. Currie gave the souvenir to Lincoln.

Q: Which president's mistress was with him at the time of his death?

A: *Franklin D. Roosevelt's.* Lucy Mercer became Eleanor Roosevelt's social secretary in 1914, when FDR served as assistant secretary of the navy. Mercer was then twenty-two years old. In 1918, Mrs. Roosevelt found love letters between Mercer and her husband and threatened Franklin with divorce. Roosevelt promised to end the affair, and Mercer married Winthrop Rutherfurd in 1920. But unbeknownst to Mrs. Roosevelt, the relationship continued. Mercer frequently visited the president at the White House when Mrs. Roosevelt was away. She was with the president in Warm Springs, Georgia, when he died suddenly in 1945.

Q: Who is the only president buried in Washington's National Cathedral?

Woodrow Wilson. The former president died on February 3, 1924, just hours after declaring, "I am a broken piece of machinery … I am ready." There was no state funeral, but services were held at his home and at the Bethlehem Chapel of National Cathedral. The cathedral has been the site of many funerals and memorial services for presidents, but Wilson remains the only president actually buried there.

Q: Who was the first president to have full-time Secret Service protection?

A: *Theodore Roosevelt.* Roosevelt became president on the death of William McKinley. McKinley had been attending the Pan-American Exposition in Buffalo when he was shot by a man—Leon Czolgosz—who had patiently waited in line to greet him. Originally created in 1865 to safeguard the nation's currency, the Secret Service was assigned responsibility for the president's personal safety after the fatal attack on McKinley.

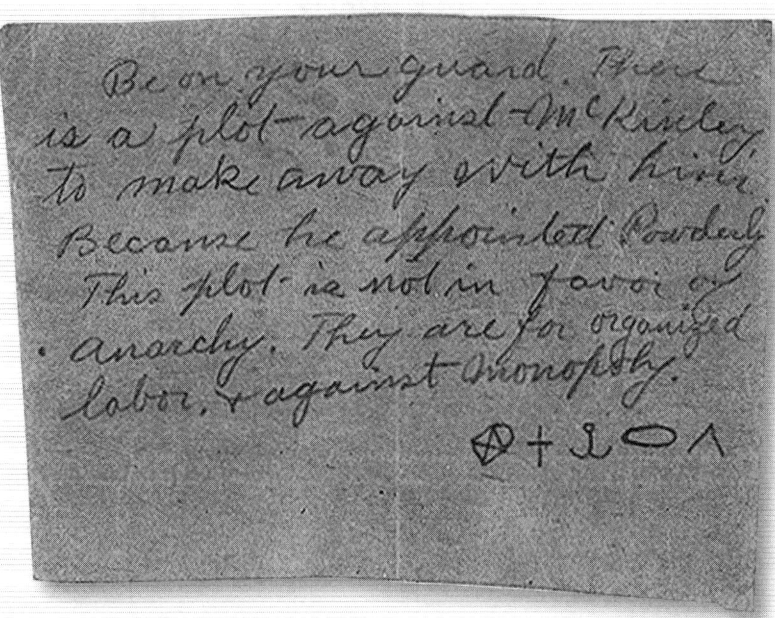

Be on your guard. There is a plot against McKinley to make away with him. Because he appointed Powderly. This plot is not in favor of anarchy. They are for organized labor, & against monopoly.

Note warning McKinley's security of a threat against the president, 1897.

Q: Which presidents shared the same pall (cloth used to cover the coffin)?

A: *Abraham Lincoln and James Garfield.* Yes, the phrase "casts a pall" comes from the pall—or cover—that drapes a coffin. The same silk cloth that was draped over Lincoln's coffin in 1865, when his body lay in state in Cleveland, Ohio, was also used on Garfield's coffin in 1881. Both presidents were assassinated.

Black silk cloth draped over the coffins of both Lincoln (1865) and Garfield (1881).

Q: Which president's assassination was the first to be widely reported on national television?

A: *John F. Kennedy's.* On Friday, November 22, 1963, regularly scheduled TV programs were interrupted by news bulletins reporting that the president's motorcade had been fired on in Dallas, Texas. The fate of the president was not immediately known and the press waited anxiously at Parkland Hospital for word of his condition. Finally, CBS News anchor Walter Cronkite, struggling for composure, came on the air and announced that Kennedy had died. With the public reeling from shock and sadness, the three networks suspended regular schedules to air a marathon of assassination coverage that ended with the president's burial at Arlington National Cemetery on Monday, November 25.

Q: Who was the first vice president to ascend to the presidency after a president's death?

A: *John Tyler.* Vice President Tyler was not kept in the loop about William Henry Harrison's declining health, so when President Harrison finally succumbed to pneumonia a month after taking the oath of office, Tyler was stunned to find himself with the top job. On hearing of Harrison's death, he immediately set out from his Williamsburg, Virginia, home for Washington. He was sworn in on April 6, 1841. As the first to ascend to the presidency without being elected, Tyler was nicknamed His Accidency.

Chapter **10**

Presidents and the Popular Imagination

ITEMS THAT CELEBRATE AND MYTHOLOGIZE OUR COUNTRY'S LEADERS

"I don't think my name is likely to be worth much in the bear business, but you're welcome to use it."

—*Teddy Roosevelt to Morris Mitchom, creator of the Teddy Bear*

Q: **What popular stuffed toy was named for a president?**

A: *The Teddy Bear.* The adventurous Theodore "Teddy" Roosevelt was a great outdoorsman and loved to hunt. However, a 1902 newspaper cartoon by Clifford Berryman showed the president in a different light. In Berryman's drawing, Roosevelt refuses to shoot a defenseless bear cub that had been captured and held by a rope. Based on a true incident, the cartoon showed the kinder, gentler side of Roosevelt. Inspired by Berryman's cartoon, Morris Mitchom created the first Teddy Bear, and his brainstorm was such a success that it led to the founding of the Ideal Novelty and Toy Company. One of the first Teddy Bears lives at the Smithsonian.

One of the first Teddy Bears, produced by the Ideal Novelty and Toy Company, 1903.

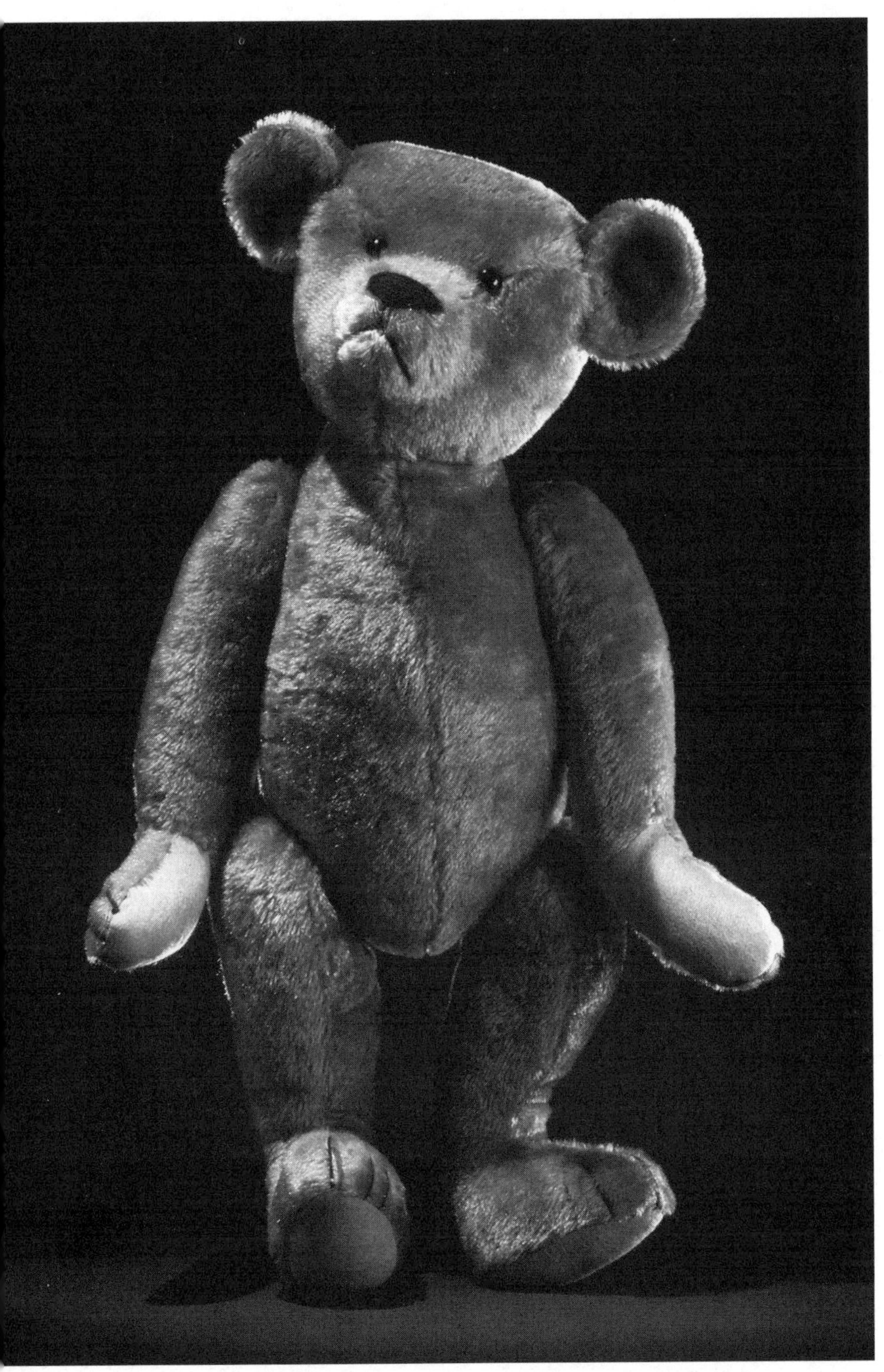

Q: Which twentieth-century first lady became a fashion trendsetter and cultural icon?

A: *Jacqueline Kennedy.* Whether outfitted in suits by designers Oleg Cassini and Coco Chanel, or dressed in gowns by Dior and Givenchy, Kennedy created a sensation. Her European-inspired wardrobe made her a fashion icon in the sixties, and soon American women were rushing out to buy copies of her trademark pillbox hats, low-heeled pumps, and sleeveless A-line dresses. Along with notched-collar jackets and triple-stranded pearls, these items constituted what became known as the Jackie Look.

Jackie Kennedy's silk brocade suit, designed by Oleg Cassini, 1961.

Q: How many presidents have said "Live from New York, it's Saturday night!" on *Saturday Night Live*?

A: *One: Gerald Ford.* Ford made a cameo appearance on *Saturday Night Live* (then known as *NBC's Saturday Night*) during the show's first season, on April 17, 1976, when his press secretary Ron Nessen hosted the show. The popular comedy show had been mercilessly lampooning the president for months. Comedian Chevy Chase parodied Ford as a hopeless klutz who stumbled across the Oval Office and hit his head on the presidential podium when giving a speech. Ford, who was actually a nimble athlete in his youth, did not seem offended.

Q: Who was the first president portrayed in a commercial film?

A: *Abraham Lincoln.* Lincoln has been represented in more than 150 films, making him the most frequently portrayed president. One of the first representations of Lincoln in a movie was in the classic *Birth of a Nation*, directed by D. W. Griffith in 1915. The film is set during and just after the Civil War and is basically a pro-South and often blatantly racist version of events, but it shows Lincoln as a compassionate leader and a symbol of hope, until his assassination throws the nation into chaos.

Q: For which president was the first presidential library founded?

A: *Franklin D. Roosevelt.* Roosevelt believed that presidential papers were an important part of the nation's history. He donated his personal and presidential records to the federal government in 1939 and asked the National Archives to administer his library. Harry Truman followed suit in 1950, and in 1955 Congress passed the Presidential Libraries Act, establishing a system of private libraries under federal supervision. There are now thirteen presidential libraries in the system.

Q: Which presidents are celebrated on Mount Rushmore?

A: *George Washington, Thomas Jefferson, Abraham Lincoln, and Theodore Roosevelt.* This grand presidential tourist attraction in the Black Hills of South Dakota was the brainchild of historian Jonah LeRoy "Doane" Robinson. With the support of Senator Peter Norbeck and the skill of sculptor Gutzon Borglum, it became a reality. Borglum chose to carve the heads of Washington, Jefferson, Lincoln, and Roosevelt because he wanted to draw visitors from across the nation. It took from October 1927 to October 1941 to turn the mountain into a monumental work of art. Millions now trek to the site each year to see this shrine to American history.

Q: Which presidential wedding inspired a wealth of advertising and commemorative material?

A: *Grover Cleveland's.* The first president to wed in the White House was Cleveland and his twenty-one-year-old bride, who was twenty-eight years younger than he. Their wedding started a media frenzy. The likeness of beautiful Frances Folsom appeared in newspapers and magazines; on plates, sheet music, and playing cards; and in a variety of advertisements—all produced without her permission.

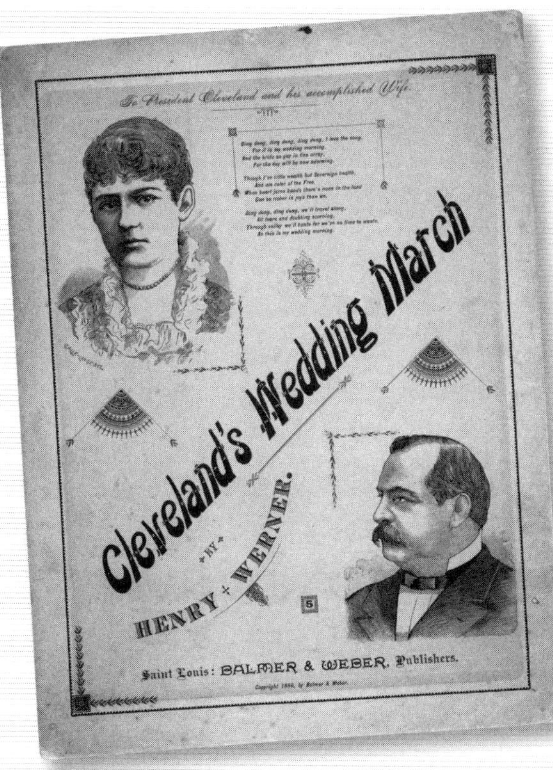

A wedding march inspired by Cleveland's young bride, published by Balmer and Weber, 1886.

Q: **What president's birthplace is celebrated in a best-selling building set for children?**

A: *Abraham Lincoln's log cabin.* One of the most successful toys associated with the presidency is Lincoln Logs, which lets children build log cabins that look the way the public imagined the early home of Lincoln. John Lloyd Wright, son of renowned architect Frank Lloyd Wright, invented Lincoln Logs in 1916.

The "all-American" Lincoln Logs created by John Lloyd Wright, 1916.

Q: Which president uttered a legendary punch line as a guest on a popular TV show ?

A: *Richard Nixon.* During the September 16, 1968, episode of the popular show *Laugh-In*, Nixon, then a candidate for president, appeared for a few seconds. He participated in a common gag on the show called "sock it to me." Generally the "sock it to me" person was doused with water, but Nixon did not suffer that indignity. An invitation to be on the show was also extended to Nixon's opponent, Vice President Hubert Humphrey, but he declined. The public must have liked seeing the lighter side of Nixon, who won the election two months later.

Q: Which president is memorialized by a university that he founded and designed?

A: *Thomas Jefferson.* A great scholar himself, Jefferson believed that a good education was essential to citizens in a democracy. To that end, he founded the University of Virginia and arranged everything from the physical site of the institution and architecture of the buildings, to the planning of the curriculum and hiring of the teachers. The third president was so proud of this achievement that he chose to mention it when writing the epitaph for his tombstone.

Q: Which president's reputation as an adventurer was used to sell travelers checks?

A: *Theodore Roosevelt.* In the early twentieth century, Roosevelt's image was popular among advertisers. His vigor, enthusiastic personality, and credibility as both president and war hero lent legitimacy to any product. Roosevelt's reputation as an international adventurer was used to sell ABA Travelers Cheques. The ad boasts that when Roosevelt went on his famous South American expedition in 1913–14 he carried ABA Travelers Cheques.

Ad for ABA Travelers Cheques, endorsed by adventurer Roosevelt after he left the White House.

Q: Which presidents are celebrated by memorials on or near the National Mall in Washington, D.C.?

A: *George Washington, Abraham Lincoln, Thomas Jefferson, Ulysses S. Grant, and Franklin D. Roosevelt.* The National Mall and Memorial Parks comprise more than 1,000 acres of parkland in Washington, D.C. The area includes the Washington Monument, Thomas Jefferson Memorial, Lincoln Memorial, Franklin Delano Roosevelt Memorial, and Ulysses S. Grant Memorial. Because it is the nation's capital, the city of Washington, D.C., is by its very existence a tribute to all the nation's presidents. And it is named for the first man to hold the office.

Q: Which "first baby" had a candy bar named in her honor?

A: *Ruth Cleveland.* The Baby Ruth candy bar, introduced in the early 1920s by Curtiss Candy Company, is ostensibly named after President Grover Cleveland's daughter Ruth. The trademark was patterned after the engraved lettering used on a medallion struck for the 1893 Chicago World's Columbian Exposition. The image pictured the President, his wife, and young daughter Baby Ruth. But Cleveland's daughter died in 1904, and the debut of the candy bar coincided with baseball legend Babe Ruth's rise to fame, leading to speculation that the company simply didn't want to pay the slugger any royalties for use of his name.

Q: Which president and his family were the first to be satirized on a popular, commercially distributed record album?

A: *John F. Kennedy. The First Family*, which parodied Kennedy as both the country's leader and a member of a large political family, was released in late 1962. Comedian and impersonator Vaughn Meader played Kennedy and had the president's Boston accent down to a T. The album sold more than a million copies in its first week and more than seven million in just a few months. *The First Family* won a Grammy Award for album of the year in 1963, but after the sad news of Kennedy's assassination, the producers stopped distribution of the record and destroyed all unsold copies.

Meader's spoof on the Kennedy White House, released in 1962.

THE FIRST FAMILY
FEATURING
VAUGHN MEADER
WITH
EARLE DOUD ~ NAOMI BROSSART ~ BOB BOOKER ~ NORMA MACMILLA
CADENCE CLP 3060

Q: Which president wrote the first presidential memoir?

A: *James Buchanan.* History has not been kind to Buchanan, whose ineptitude in office contributed to the outbreak of the Civil War. But he does have a "first" to his name. In 1866, he wrote the first presidential memoir, titled *Mr. Buchanan's Administration on the Eve of Rebellion*. The book was an attempt to defend his administration and shift blame for secession to others. It was not a top seller in its time.

Q: Which president has never been the leading character in a major motion picture, although he has been represented in minor roles in many movies?

A: *George Washington.* The presidency has been an element of feature films from the beginning, although movies depicting actual presidents have rarely been box-office successes. Some films have sought to glorify the men in the Oval Office; others have turned the president into an action hero, a romantic figure, or a symbol of all that is right or wrong in America. But Washington has always had a bit part. Although he is the Father of Our Country, he's no leading man.

Q: Who was the first sitting president to be portrayed as a main character in a Broadway play?

A: *Franklin D. Roosevelt.* George M. Cohan played Roosevelt in *I'd Rather Be Right*, which debuted on Broadway in 1937. Instead of impersonating the wheelchair-bound FDR, Cohan gave an all-out song and dance performance. No one had ever depicted a sitting president in a musical before, so *I'd Rather Be Right* opened amid extraordinary press hoopla. Critics raved, Roosevelt (a longtime fan of Cohan's) expressed his approval, and the show became the hottest ticket on Broadway.

Q: The Library of Congress has three buildings named after which three presidents?

A: *Thomas Jefferson, John Adams, and James Madison.* Founded in 1800, the Library of Congress is the national library of the United States. After its holdings were burned during the War of 1812, the library purchased books from Jefferson's personal library, which became the core of the collection. The first permanent building to house the library was named for Jefferson and opened in 1897. The John Adams Building was opened in 1939, and the James Madison Building came later in 1981. The library not only serves Congress, but also is a resource for researchers and scholars.

Q: Which president supported a bill that would prevent commercial use of celebrities' names and images without their written consent?

A: *Grover Cleveland.* Cleveland's wife, Frances, brought youth, beauty, and style to the White House. Her name and likeness appeared on everyday items from candy, perfume, face cream, and liver pills, to ashtrays and women's undergarments. One Democratic congressman attempted to pass a bill in Congress that would halt the use of any woman's image for commercial purposes without her written permission—and it had the president's support. But the bill failed to come up for a vote in the House, which made Frances fair game for every enterprising slogan writer and salesman in town.

Playing cards with the president as king, Frances as queen, and running mate Allen Thurman as jack, 1888.

Q: Which president was known as the Railsplitter?

A:

Abraham Lincoln. Lincoln had many jobs as a young man, including splitting rails. During his presidential campaign, supporters emphasized Honest Abe's humble origins by carrying symbols such as wooden axes in campaign rallies and parades. A precious Lincoln rail-splitting relic came to the Smithsonian in 1984. Though it looks like any weathered piece of wood, it is actually a piece of a fence rail split by Abraham Lincoln in 1829 or 1830. It came with a letter of authenticity from John Hanks, Lincoln's cousin.

Piece of a fence rail split by Lincoln and 1860 letter attesting to its authenticity.

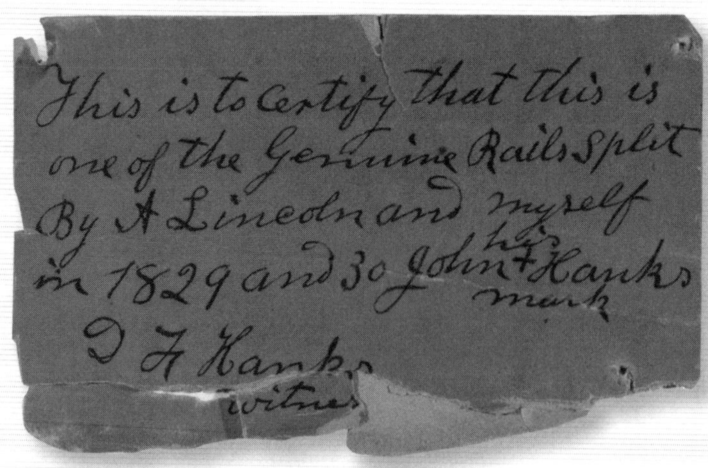

This is to certify that this is
one of the Genuine Rails Split
By A Lincoln and myself
in 1829 and 30 John his + mark Hanks
D F Hanks
witness

Chapter 11

The Quotable President

QUIPS, SOUND BITES, AND STATEMENTS BY THOSE WHO HAVE HELD THE OFFICE

"If one morning I walked on top of the water across the Potomac River, the headline that afternoon would read, 'President Can't Swim.' "

—*Lyndon B. Johnson*

Guess which presidents said the following:

1. "Being a president is like riding a tiger. A man has to keep on riding or be swallowed."
2. "In our progress toward political happiness my station is new; and, if I may use the expression, I walk on untrodden ground."
3. "No man is good enough to govern another man, without the other's consent."
4. "The pen is mightier than the politician."
5. "The presidency has made every man who occupied it, no matter how small, bigger than he was; and no matter how big, not big enough for its demands."
6. "I hate war as only a soldier who has lived it can, only as one who has seen it brutality, its futility, its stupidity."
7. "In a body where there are more than one hundred talking lawyers … you can make no calculation upon the termination of any debate and frequently, the more trifling the subject, the more animated and protracted the discussion."
8. "I may be president of the United States, but my private life is nobody's business."
9. "If you want to make enemies, try to change something."
10. "Retired. Glad of it."

1. Harry Truman; **2.** George Washington; **3.** Abraham Lincoln; **4.** Gerald Ford; **5.** Lyndon Johnson; **6.** Dwight Eisenhower; **7.** Franklin Pierce, *commenting on Congress*; **8.** Chester Arthur; **9.** Woodrow Wilson; **10.** Calvin Coolidge, *on a card accompanying a payment to the National Press Club, which asked for "occupation" and "remarks."*

11. "I pray Heaven to bestow the best of Blessings on this House and all that shall hereafter inhabit it. May none but honest and wise Men ever rule under this roof."

12. "Change will not come if we wait for some other person or some other time. We are the ones we've been waiting for. We are the change that we seek."

13. "I only have two regrets: I didn't shoot Henry Clay, and I didn't hang John C. Calhoun."

14. "I have no trouble with my enemies. I can take care of my enemies all right. But my damn friends, my goddamn friends, they're the ones that keep me walking the floor nights."

15. "My dear sir, if you are as happy on entering the White House as I am on leaving it, you are a very happy man indeed."

16. "Well, I am heartily tired of this life of bondage, responsibility, and toil."

17. "No man who ever held the office of president would congratulate a friend on obtaining it. He will make one man ungrateful, and a hundred men his enemies, for every office he can bestow."

18. "No man will ever bring out of that office the reputation which carries him into it."

19. "I don't remember that I ever was president."

11. John Adams, *writing on his second night at the White House*; **12.** Barack Obama, *in a speech on Feb. 5, 2008*; **13.** Andrew Jackson, *about his political opponents*; **14.** Warren Harding, *in the midst of a variety of scandals*; **15.** James Buchanan, *to Abraham Lincoln*; **16.** Rutherford B. Hayes; **17.** John Adams; **18.** Thomas Jefferson; **19.** William Howard Taft, *on becoming chief justice of the Supreme Court.*

20. “Well, there doesn’t seem to be anything else for an ex-president to do but go into the country and raise big pumpkins.”

21. “Boys, if you ever pray, pray for me now.”

22. “I’ve noticed that nothing I’ve never said has hurt me.”

23. “Being president is like being a jackass in a hailstorm. There’s nothing to do but stand there and take it.”

24. “I guess it just proves that in America, anyone can be president.”

25. “This office is a sacred trust and I am determined to be worthy of that trust.”

26. “For too long we’ve been told about ‘us’ and ‘them.’ Each and every election we see a new slate of arguments and ads telling us that ‘they’ are the problem, not ‘us.’ But there can be no ‘them’ in America. There’s only us.”

27. “How can a president not be an actor?”

28. “All men having power ought to be mistrusted.”

20. Chester Arthur; **21.** Harry Truman, *to reporters on the day after becoming president (April 13, 1945)*; **22.** Calvin Coolidge; **23.** Lyndon B. Johnson; **24.** Gerald Ford; **25.** Richard Nixon, *in the midst of the Watergate scandal*; **26.** Bill Clinton; **27.** Ronald Reagan; **28.** James Madison.

Presidential Timeline

Quick facts about America's chief executives

1. George Washington
Born: February 22, 1732, Westmoreland County, Virginia
Died: December 14, 1799
Term:1789–1797
Vice President: John Adams

2. John Adams
Born: October 30, 1735, Braintree, Massachusetts
Died: July 4, 1826
Term:1797–1801
Vice President: Thomas Jefferson

3. Thomas Jefferson
Born: April 13, 1743, Albemarle County, Virginia
Died: July 4, 1826
Term:1801–1809
Vice Presidents: Aaron Burr (1801–1805); George Clinton (1805–1809)

4. James Madison
Born: March 16, 1751, Port Conway, Virginia
Died: June 28, 1836
Term: 1809–1817
Vice Presidents: George Clinton (1809–1812); Elbridge Gerry (1813–1814)

5. James Monroe
Born: April 28, 1758, Westmoreland County, Virginia
Died: July 4, 1831
Term: 1817–1825
Vice President: Daniel Tompkins

6. John Quincy Adams
Born: July 11, 1767, Braintree, Massachusetts
Died: February 23, 1848
Term:1825–1829
Vice President: John Calhoun

7. Andrew Jackson
Born: March 15, 1767, Waxhaw settlement, South Carolina
Died: June 8, 1845
Term: 1829–1837
Vice Presidents: John Calhoun (1829–1832);
Martin Van Buren (1833–1837)

8. Martin Van Buren
Born: December 5, 1782, Kinderhook, New York
Died: July 24, 1862
Term: 1837–1841
Vice President: Richard Johnson

9. William Henry Harrison
Born: February 9, 1773, Berkeley, Virginia
Died: April 4, 1841
Term: 1841
Vice President: John Tyler

10. John Tyler
Born: March 29, 1790, Charles City County, Virginia
Died: January 18, 1862
Term: 1841–1845
Vice President: None

11. James Polk
Born: November 2, 1795, Mecklenburg County, North Carolina
Died: June 15, 1849
Term: 1845–1849
Vice President: George Dallas

12. Zachary Taylor
Born: November 24, 1784, Orange County, Virginia
Died: July 9, 1850
Term: 1849–1850
Vice President: Millard Fillmore

13. Millard Fillmore
Born: January 7, 1800, Locke, New York
Died: March 8, 1874
Term: 1850–1853
Vice President: None

14. Franklin Pierce
Born: November 23, 1804, Hillsborough, New Hampshire
Died: October 8, 1869
Term: 1853–1857
Vice President: William King (1853); None (1853–1857)

15. James Buchanan
Born: April 23, 1791, Cove Gap, Pennsylvania
Died: June 1, 1868
Term: 1857–1861
Vice President: John Breckinridge

16. Abraham Lincoln
Born: February 12, 1809, near Hodgenville, Kentucky
Died: April 15, 1865
Term: 1861–1865
Vice Presidents: Hannibal Hamlin (1861–1865); Andrew Johnson (1865)

17. Andrew Johnson
Born: December 29, 1808, Raleigh, North Carolina
Died: July 31, 1875
Term: 1865–1869
Vice President: None

18. Ulysses S. Grant
Born: April 27, 1822, Point Pleasant, Ohio
Died: July 23, 1885
Term: 1869–1877
Vice Presidents: Schuyler Colfax (1869–1873); Henry Wilson (1873–1875); None (1875–1877)

19. Rutherford B. Hayes
Born: October 4, 1822, Delaware, Ohio.
Died: January 17, 1893
Term: 1877–1881
Vice President: William Wheeler

20. James Garfield
Born: November 19, 1831, Orange, Ohio
Died: September 19, 1881
Term: 1881
Vice President: Chester Arthur

21. Chester Arthur

Born: October 5, 1829, Fairfield, Vermont.
Died: November 18, 1886
Term: 1881–1885
Vice President: None

22. Grover Cleveland

Born: March 18, 1837, Caldwell, New Jersey
Died: June 24, 1908
Term: 1885–1889
Vice President: Thomas Hendricks (1885); None (1885–1889)

23. Benjamin Harrison

Born: August 20, 1833, North Bend, Ohio
Died: March 13, 1901
Term: 1889–1893
Vice President: Levi Morton

24. Grover Cleveland

Born: March 18, 1837, Caldwell, New Jersey.
Died: June 24, 1908
Terms: 1893–1897
Vice President: Adlai Stevenson

25. William McKinley

Born: January 29, 1843, Niles, Ohio.
Died: September 14, 1901
Term: 1897–1901
Vice Presidents: Garret Hobart (1897–1899); None (1899–1901); Theodore Roosevelt (1901)

26. Theodore Roosevelt

Born: October 27, 1858, New York, New York
Died: January 6, 1919
Term: 1901–1909
Vice President: Charles Fairbanks

27. William Howard Taft

Born: September 15, 1857, Cincinnati, Ohio
Died: March 8, 1930
Term: 1909–1913
Vice President: James Sherman (1909–1912); None (1912–1913)

28. Woodrow Wilson
Born: December 28, 1856, Staunton, Virginia
Died: February 3, 1924
Term: 1913–1921
Vice President: Thomas Marshall

29. Warren Harding
Born: November 2, 1865, near Blooming Grove, Ohio
Died: August 2, 1923
Term: 1921–1923
Vice President: Calvin Coolidge

30. Calvin Coolidge
Born: July 4, 1872, Plymouth Notch, Vermont
Died: January 5, 1933
Term: 1923–1929
Vice President: None (1923–1925); Charles Dawes (1925–1929)

31. Herbert Hoover
Born: August 10, 1874, West Branch, Iowa
Died: October 20, 1964
Term: 1929–1933
Vice President: Charles Curtis

32. Franklin D. Roosevelt
Born: January 30, 1882, Hyde Park, New York
Died: April 12, 1945
Term: 1933–1945
Vice Presidents: John Garner (1933–1941);
Henry Wallace (1941–1945); Harry Truman (1945)

33. Harry Truman
Born: May 8, 1884, Lamar, Missouri
Died: December 26, 1972
Term: 1945–1953
Vice President: None (1945–1949); Alben Barkley (1949–1953)

34. Dwight Eisenhower
Born: October 14, 1890, Denison, Texas
Died: March 28, 1969
Term: 1953–1961
Vice President: Richard Nixon

35. John F. Kennedy
Born: May 29, 1917, Brookline, Massachusetts
Died: November 22, 1963
Term: 1961–1963
Vice President: Lyndon Johnson

36. Lyndon Johnson
Born: August 27, 1908, near Stonewall, Texas
Died: January 22, 1973
Term: 1963–1969
Vice President: None (1963–1965); Hubert Humphrey (1965–1969)

37. Richard Nixon
Born: January 9, 1913, Yorba Linda, California
Died: April 22, 1994
Term: 1969–1974
Vice Presidents: Spiro Agnew (1969–1973); Gerald Ford (1973–1974)

38. Gerald Ford
Born: July 14, 1913, Omaha, Nebraska
Died: December 26, 2006
Term: 1974–1977
Vice President: Nelson Rockefeller

39. Jimmy Carter
Born: October 1, 1924, Plains, Georgia
Term: 1977–1981
Vice President: Walter Mondale

40. Ronald Reagan
Born: February 6, 1911, Tampico, Illinois
Died: June 5, 2004
Term: 1981–1989
Vice President: George H. W. Bush

41. George H. W. Bush
Born: June 12, 1924, Milton, Massachusetts
Term: 1989–1993
Vice President: Dan Quayle

42. Bill Clinton

Born: August 19, 1946, Hope, Arkansas
Term: 1993–2001
Vice President: Al Gore

43. George W. Bush

Born: July 6, 1946, New Haven, Connecticut
Term: 2001–2009
Vice President: Dick Cheney

44. Barack Obama

Born: August 4, 1961, Honolulu, Hawaii
Term: 2009–
Vice President: Joe Biden

Photography Credits

All photographs are courtesy of the Smithsonian National Museum of American History except for the following:

Cover, background: ©Ocean/Corbis; **Theodore Roosevelt:** Library of Congress, Prints & Photographs Division; **page 12:** Courtesy of the Supreme Court; **page 87:** Library of Congress, Prints & Photographs Division; **page 118:** Library of Congress, Prints & Photographs Division; **page 127:** Library of Congress, Prints & Photographs Division; **page 132:** ©Bettmann/Corbis; **page 141:** Library of Congress, Prints & Photographs Division; **page 150:** Library of Congress, Prints & Photographs Division; **page 156:** Library of Congress, Prints & Photographs Division; **page 160:** Library of Congress, Prints & Photographs Division; **page 163:** Library of Congress, Prints & Photographs Division; **page 169:** Time & Life Pictures/Getty Images; **page 172:** ©Corbis; **page 175:** Library of Congress, Prints & Photographs Division; **page 184:** Museum of the City of New York; **page 233:** Washington: National Portrait Gallery, Smithsonian Institution; John Adams: White House Historical Association; Jefferson: White House Historical Association; Madison: White House Historical Association; Monroe: White House Historical Association; John Quincy Adams: Library of Congress, Prints & Photographs Division; **page 234:** Jackson: White House Historical Association; Van Buren: Library of Congress, Prints & Photographs Division; William Henry Harrison: Library of Congress, Prints & Photographs Division; Tyler: National Portrait Gallery, Smithsonian Institution; Polk: Library of Congress, Prints & Photographs Division; Taylor: Library of Congress, Prints & Photographs Division; Fillmore: Library of Congress, Prints & Photographs Division; **page 235:** Pierce: National Portrait Gallery, Smithsonian Institution; Buchanan: Library of Congress, Prints & Photographs Division; Lincoln: Library of Congress, Prints & Photographs Division; Andrew Johnson: Library of Congress, Prints & Photographs Division; Grant: Library of Congress, Prints & Photographs Division; Hayes: National Portrait Gallery, Smithsonian Institution; Garfield: Library of Congress, Prints & Photographs Division; **page 236:** Arthur: National Portrait Gallery, Smithsonian Institution; Cleveland: Library of Congress, Prints & Photographs Division; Benjamin Harrison: Library of Congress, Prints & Photographs Division; Cleveland: Library of Congress, Prints & Photographs Division; McKinley: Library of Congress, Prints & Photographs Division; Theodore Roosevelt: Library of Congress, Prints & Photographs Division; Taft: Library of Congress, Prints & Photographs Division; **page 237:** Wilson: Library of Congress, Prints & Photographs Division; Harding: Library of Congress, Prints & Photographs Division; Coolidge: Library of Congress, Prints & Photographs Division; Hoover: Library of Congress, Prints & Photographs Division; Franklin D. Roosevelt: Library of Congress, Prints & Photographs Division; Truman: Harry S. Truman Library; Eisenhower: White House Historical Association; **page 238:** Kennedy: Library of Congress, Prints & Photographs Division; Lyndon Johnson: Library of Congress, Prints & Photographs Division; Nixon: The National Archives; Ford: Courtesy Gerald R. Ford Library; Carter: Library of Congress, Prints & Photographs Division; Reagan: Library of Congress, Prints & Photographs Division; George H. W. Bush: White House Historical Association; **page 239:** Clinton: Library of Congress, Prints & Photographs Division; George W. Bush: Courtesy of the George W. Bush Presidential Library; Obama: Library of Congress, Prints & Photographs Division.